Self-Management and Self-Marketing

*A strategic approach
to employability skills development*

Valeri Chukhlomin

*State University of New York
Empire State College*

Self-Management and Self-Marketing:

A strategic approach to employability skills development

Valeri Chukhlomin, PhD

Saratoga Springs, New York

Self-Management and Self-Marketing:
A strategic approach to employability skills development
112 p.

ISBN-13: 978-1500837785
ISBN-10: 1500837784

Contents

Preface

Currently, there is a growing understanding of the necessity to embed competencies and skill-building into the design of undergraduate and graduate degrees, particularly within the business and management environment. This book is intended for senior undergraduate and graduate students specializing in any area of business, management and economics, as it will help them better understand processes of self- and professional development and master necessary skills, such as gathering evidence, conducting self-assessment, making sense of its findings, and developing strategies for self-improvement and self-marketing. Studying it can be beneficial for managers and policy makers, as it is research-based and can provide insights into recent trends in workforce development in a global context.

This book is designed to help students achieve the following learning goals:

- Learn how to approach and conduct self-analysis, self-assessment, self-marketing and self-development in a business context;

- Implement strategic approach and use proven business strategy techniques for their professional development;

- Identify professional and generic competencies and skills that are most valuable for their chosen field; collect evidence of their actual performance, measure it against benchmarks, and learn how to monitor progress;

- Use self-management tools, such as self-assessment instruments, dashboards, e-portfolios;

- Integrate self-management and self-marketing techniques;

- Develop/deepen active learning, metacognitive and self-regulatory skills;

- Get familiar with and learn how to use underpinning learning theories, such as self-regulated learning and transformative learning, to guide their professional development and personal growth.

Since 2014, the instructional materials included in this book have been used by students conducting educational planning at the State University of New York's Empire State College (ESC). A unique approach to educational planning developed in that college provides students with an excellent opportunity to combine skill-building activities with curricular mapping and other degree planning and developmental activities. It has been proved that conducting an educational planning study within the business, management and economics (BME) area, with an emphasis on employability skills, invigorates students' interest in critical self-reflection and self-directed learning. Additionally, with the arrival of e-portfolios, such as Mahara, there is a new, powerful and versatile tool that is used by ESC students to build and strengthen their career development plans.

The book has been structured around a typical, 15-week semester course delivered either fully online or in a blended format. We recommend that it is divided into six modules:

- Module 1 introduces and examines self-management in the context of employability skills (two weeks);

- Module 2 deals with strategic self-analysis (three weeks);

- Module 3 examines approaches to self-assessment (three weeks);

- Module 4 helps to make sense of self-assessment to inform and guide self-management (three weeks);

- Module 5 examines approaches to self-marketing (three weeks);

- Module 6 closes the loop with self-reflection and planning for improvement (two weeks).

Each Module will contain a set of learning activities that may include: 1) attending a lecture and reading a content guide and recommended articles; 2) participating in a workshop or an academic discussion; 3) working independently on an e-portfolio task; 4) submitting a written assignment. Requirements and recommendations for fulfilling e-portfolio tasks are specified in the E- Portfolio and Learning Journal Workbook template.

I believe that you will find this book useful and rewarding. You will be developing and strengthening your existing skills as well as discovering areas for improvement; in addition, you'll be able to stay in control by using a benchmarking tool and a dashboard.

Valeri Chukhlomin
State University of New York Empire State College
May 2015

Acknowledgements

I would like to express my sincere gratitude to my colleagues at the ESC's Center for Distançe Learning for their support and encouragement. Particularly, I would like to mention the input from Dr. John Beckem and Suzanne Benno for their excellent ideas for student engagement. I am also indebted to the following reviewers for their comments and suggestions: Dr. Ronnie Mather and Professor Susan Oaks, State University of New York Empire State College.

About the author

Valeri (Val) Chukhlomin is Associate Professor and Academic Area Coordinator in the Center for Distance Learning at the State University of New York's Empire State College in Saratoga Springs, New York. Prior to joining SUNY in 2006, he lived and worked in Australia and Russia where he was Vice-President for Commercial and International Affairs, Dean of the School of International Business and Department Chair of Economics and Marketing at Omsk State University.

With a PhD in Political Economy, Val is an expert in international business, strategic and cross-cultural management, international education, and online learning environments. His most recent interests include international online learning, global competencies and employability skills development. Val's publications and presentations are available on his website at: http://commons.esc.edu/valerichukhlomin.

Content guides

Module 1: Employability Skills

Module 1 Overview

This is a short, two week introductory Module. The overarching goal is to examine career management and employability skills and the central role self-management plays in skills acquisition.

Learning Objectives are to:

- Discuss the vital importance of developing competencies and skills in higher education graduates in the 21st century from the employers' prospective and for the economy at large;

- Introduce and define the concepts of employability and career management skills;

- Review generic, professional and meta-skills and competencies;

- Examine how modern colleges approach graduate outcomes and help students developing generic and meta-skills; also, find out about the need for graduates to develop self-management skills;

- Review specific ways of defining and fostering graduate outcomes in your College including learning goals, area of study guidelines, and educational planning requirements;

- Examine ways in which this course can be helpful for developing self-management and self-marketing skills and beneficial for students to achieve their learning and professional goals;

- Provide a brief introduction to the use of e-portfolios and explain how this approach is used in this course.

Learning Activities may include:

- Readings including this guide and recommended learning materials (some materials are quite lengthy and can be used for further reading);

- An e-portfolio task (EP1);

- A two week discussion on employability skills (D1);

- Assignment 1 (Self-Audit survey) (A1).

Schedule and due dates. See Course Schedule.

1.1. Employability skills for the 21st century

<u>Why are skills so important in the 21st century?</u>

Actually, this is a very good question, that's why we decided to leave it for discussion D1. When looking for answers, you should use business media (The Wall Street Journal, Fortune, Forbes, and The Economist) to find out about specialists' opinion on the topic and then formulate your own judgment. Throughout this course, we'll be relying on results obtained by researchers in this and other countries to substantiate and illustrate our statements and provide you with food for thought. For example, to understand the most recent emphasis on skills and skill gaps, we recommend you reading an excellent article by Denise Jackson "An international profile of industry-relevant competencies and skill gaps in modern graduates" published by *International Journal of Management Education*, 2009, vol. 8(3), pp. 29-58.

When suggesting an article for reading, we'll be providing you with a link that is supposed to bring you to the article. But it may happen that the link will appear broken. In this case you should do the following: Open your browser and type in the browser's window <http://scholar.google.com.library.esc.edu>, then enter your college login and password and after that you'll be prompted to a Google-powered search window *inside* our College library. Then, type or copy and paste the title of the article into the search window and you'll be prompted to results. Ideally, you will see the article on top of search results. Click on it and you'll get the journal page, with a pdf of that article freely available for download (if something goes wrong, you should ask the library helpdesk to help you).

As you can see in the above article, employers across Australia, Canada, UK, US and other developed countries express concerns about growing skill gaps. Interestingly enough, according to the researchers' report employers are less concerned with gaps in discipline-specific skills and are more focused on the lack of so called basic, soft and meta-skills. You can read more about it in another article "The Future of Marketing Education: A Practitioner's Perspective" written by David Finch, John Nadeau and Norm O'Reilly for *Journal of Marketing Education*, 2013, vol. 35(1), pp. 54-67. The article that is freely available for viewing/downloading through the College online library is very interesting and well worth reading.

Here is an advice regarding reading research papers. If you do not have experience with research papers, you may think that reading 6-7 papers per week can be overwhelming. Actually, if you deal with lengthy papers, you may probably need more than a week to attentively read and fully digest just one paper. But fortunately in most cases reading can be done much faster. If you are not specifically interested in learning about the research methodology used, you can skip it and only read the abstract, introduction and findings. This won't take a lot of your time and will give you a clear idea about what the authors studied and accomplished. Sometimes, you'll need to quickly browse the paper to look for theoretical frameworks, literature review, and interim results. For example, in the above mentioned article we recommend you to review an excellent list of meta-skills compiled by the authors.

The authors of the paper studied the gap that had developed between knowledge-based curricula and practical needs and asked marketing practitioners in Canada about the gaps in education they found in recent marketing graduates. Surprisingly, those were not highly praised professional marketing skills that graduates were lacking; instead, foundational meta-skills (communication, time management, team work, problem solving, interpersonal, decision making, leadership) were found to be: a) the most desirable and valued by the employers; b) significantly underdeveloped in graduates.

Employability Skills

It is now time to more accurately define the range of skills we are dealing with. An excellent introduction to the topic was written by Anthony Carnevale, Leila Gainer and Ann Meltzer in their book "Workplace basics: The essential skills employers want"[1] (Jossey-Bass: San-Francisco, 1990). Written 25 years ago, this is still one of the best sources on employability skills. A more recent research has been undertaken by the Business Council of Australia and the Australian Chamber of Commerce and Industry which resulted in developing a framework for employability skills[2] (DEST, 2002). The authors of the report identified personal attributes required for today's employees and came up with a list of eight employability skills.

'Employability skills are defined as skills required not only to gain employment, but also to progress within an enterprise so as to achieve one's potential and contribute successfully to enterprise strategic directions.' (DEST, 2002)

The eight identified skills that were found to be the most relevant to both entry-level and established employees were the following:

- **Communication skills** that contribute to productive and harmonious relations between employees and customers;

- **Teamwork skills** that contribute to productive working relationships and outcomes;

- **Problem solving skills** that contribute to productive outcomes;

- **Self-management skills** that contribute to employee satisfaction and growth;

- **Planning and organizing skills** that contribute to long-term and short-term strategic planning;

- **Technology skills** that contribute to effective execution of tasks;

- **Life-long learning skills** that contribute to ongoing improvement and expansion in employee and company operations and outcomes;

- **Initiative and enterprise skills** that contribute to innovative outcomes.

In more detail, the above mentioned employability skills are characterized by Denise Jackson on p. 348 in her article "Business undergraduates' perceptions of their capabilities in employability skills: Implications for industry and higher education" (*Industry and Higher Education*, 2012, Vol.26(5), October, pp. 345-356).

Professional, Generic, Self- and Career Management Skills

Employability skills are composed of both professional and generic skills. Sometimes, it is difficult to tell whether a certain skill is professional or generic (i.e., not discipline specific).

---

[1] http://files.eric.ed.gov/fulltext/ED319979.pdf
[2] http://www.voced.edu.au/content/ngv33428

Professional skills are discipline (like marketing research) and even employer specific (for example, particular software, standards, customer base, etc.); they are transferrable within a company or between similar positions in different companies. A certain skill is generic if it is transferable to areas outside a particular position, company or even industry. Generic skills typically include information management, communication, interpersonal, cross-cultural, analytical and problem solving, and self-management skills. Employability skills can be analyzed at different levels (basic employability skills, graduate employability skills, career management skills). You may find useful a more detailed discussion of skills provided by Ruth Bridgestock in her article "The graduate attributes we've overlooked: enhancing graduate employability through career management skills" (*Higher Education Research and Development*, 2009, vol. 28(1), pp. 31-44).

A note on terminology: competencies, skills, capabilities

You may have already noticed that terms "competency", "skill", "capability" are often used interchangeably; in the above mentioned article by Denise Jackson you can find detailed definitions and clarifications.

1.2. Graduate outcomes and self-management

College teaching and skills acquisition

College teaching, particularly in liberal arts and sciences colleges, is mostly concerned with knowledge acquisition in general education, as well as professional areas, and developing foundational generic skills, such as academic writing, information literacy and critical thinking skills, under an assumption that it is the workplace where applied professional and advanced generic skills can and should be developed. As mentioned earlier, there is a certain gap between college teaching and workplace expectations. To help students prepare for the job market, many institutions develop career resources and skill-building courses.

An example of a career center[3] is provided by Excelsior College in New York, a skill builder and capability profiler [4]is developed by Griffith University in Australia, a standing alone skill-building course in UK is described by Geoff Baker and Debra Henson in their article "Promoting employability skills development in a research intensive university" (*Education+Training*, 2010, vol. 52(1), pp. 62-75).

To increase job readiness of their graduates, some colleges currently experiment with so called "competency-based" education and assessment; a very interesting example is presented in an article written by Elaine Danneler "The Portfolio approach to competency-based assessment at the Cleveland Clinic Lerner College of Medicine" (*Academic Medicine*, Vol. 82(5), May, 2007, pp. 493-502). The idea behind competency-based education is to build the entire curriculum around assessable skills and competencies, but it appears that it is very difficult to implement this idea in an academic setting. In fact, employability skills are typically the result of many academic and training courses, as well as work-based learning and individual efforts

---

[3] http://www.excelsior.edu/web/career-center/home
[4] http://www.griffith.edu.au/careers-employment/for-students

undertaken by students. Ultimately, it is the students who are the most interested in and responsible for the development of graduate outcomes, including graduate employability skills.

College Graduate attributes

With increasing competition in higher education, nationally and globally, many universities around the globe have recognized the need for their graduates to successfully compete on the job market by demonstrating superior graduate employability skills. As a result, those universities have begun emphasizing programs that foster skill-based outcomes ("attributes"). For example, a Griffith University's list of graduate attributes[5] includes professional skills in the disciplines, as well as generic skills, such as communication skills, innovation, social responsiveness and cross-cultural competence. Those skills are mapped[6] by faculty and administrators and linked to courses throughout the curriculum. Some universities (for example, the University of Glasgow in Scotland[7]) have begun promoting self-management, lifelong and self-directed learning skills as desired graduate attributes, as it has become clear that in most occupations it now takes less than a decade for the knowledge base to become obsolete and students should be able to re-educate themselves. You can read more about graduate attributes in the above mentioned article by Ruth Bridgestock.

Career development, individual learning goals and self-management

It is likely that after completing a pre-designed program of studies built around graduate attributes students are better prepared for a reality check on the job market. But what actually happens when all classes are over and there seems to be no way for a worker to secure continuing professional growth and career development other than through self-improvement? It is logical to suggest that at some stage everyone has to learn about how to become her/his own trainer, assessor, and mentor and assume the responsibility for developing career management skills. This is where self-management skills and techniques can be very helpful.

Self-Management: a meta-skill and a strategy for self-development

From a narrow point of view, self-management is concerned with developing personal attributes, motivations, dispositions for a better self-control, and as such it is one of employability skills (DEST, 2002). In a much broader perspective, self-management is an overarching skill of self-observation, self-analysis and self-programming that is needed for any individual striving to accomplish personal and career development goals in a complex environment by mastering a range of professional and generic skills. In other words, self-management is a "meta-skill" (*meta* means "beyond"), i.e., a skill that is needed to develop other skills. Also, it is a strategic skill, because when functioning in a complex, competitive environment, an individual needs to strategically approach her/his self-development to be acutely aware of the external needs and requirements, to make sure that her/his goals are realistic, self-analysis is accurate and self-programming is adequate to reach the goals. In this course, we'll be using a broad definition of

---

[5] http://www.griffith.edu.au/learning-teaching/student-success/graduate-attributes
[6] http://www.griffith.edu.au/learning-teaching/student-success/graduate-attributes/mapping-graduate-attributes
[7] http://www.gla.ac.uk/media/media_218771_en.pdf

"self-management" as both a meta-skill and a strategy for acquisition of desired employability skills.

College Graduate outcomes, lifelong and adult learning and self-management

Colleges specializing in adult education have been promoting lifelong and self-directed learning for decades; for example, SUNY Empire State College's educational planning has become the hallmark of individualized, goal-driven progressive education[8]. As a mandatory part of the College's curriculum, it provides room for studying and developing self-management skills.

1.3. CASE STUDY: SUNY Empire State College's learning outcomes and Educational Planning

The Empire State College's approach

In SUNY ESC graduate outcomes are established on three levels. On the system (SUNY) level, all graduates are supposed to develop foundational generic skills[9], such as critical thinking, communication skills and information management skills. On the institutional level, graduates are supposed to develop learning outcomes in compliance with the College's Learning Goals[10]. One of the learning goals specifically requires students to become active learners and develop self-directed learning skills. Finally, the Area of Study (AOS) requirements specify graduate outcomes for all graduates in each particular area of study. For example, all Business, Management and Economics (BME) graduates are expected to gain knowledge and develop professional and generic skills and competencies in seven specified areas[11]. When conducting a mandatory educational (degree) planning study, all SUNY ESC students are required to address the above mentioned requirements and provide curricular mapping to demonstrate how their individual degree program (DP) including learning experiences obtained outside the College help them comply with the requirements and attain specified, as well as individual, learning goals.

 How BME-214524 connects to and goes beyond DP planning

While the above mentioned degree planning process is an excellent instrument for the identification of individual learning goals and curricular mapping in accordance with the requirements (i.e., for identifying the purpose of each study included into the student's individual DP), it doesn't provide students with a tool to monitor their progress in terms of the acquisition of graduate employability skills. The DP planning process is mostly concerned with defining what courses/studies students need to take in the College, it doesn't provide the students with a tool to measure the outcomes of their studies and doesn't inform them about the level of skills acquisition they have achieved as a result of their studies in the College. Neither it necessarily

---

[8] https://net.educause.edu/ir/library/pdf/pub720311.pdf

[9] http://www.suny.edu/student/academic_general_education.cfm

[10] http://www.esc.edu/media/academic-affairs/College-Level-Learning-Goals-1-20-2012.pdf

[11] http://www.esc.edu/degrees-programs/undergraduate-aos/business-management-economics/bme-guidelines/matriculated-effective-2004-jan-1/

tells them about next logical steps in professional development, nor does it provide with a valid self-management technique.

BME-214524 is a course that is a logical extension of educational planning; it builds on the degree planning process and goes beyond it. In particular, in this course students:

- Learn how to approach and conduct self-analysis, self-assessment, self-marketing and self-development in a business context;

- Implement strategic approach and use proven business strategy techniques for their professional development;

- Identify professional and generic competencies and skills that are most valuable for their chosen field; collect evidence of their actual performance, measure it against benchmarks, and learn how to evaluate and monitor progress;

- Use self-management tools, such as self-assessment instruments, dashboards, e-portfolios;

- Integrate self-management and self-marketing techniques;

- Develop/deepen active learning, metacognitive and self-regulatory skills;

- Get familiar with and learn how to use underpinning learning theories, such as self-regulated learning, to guide their professional development and personal growth.

How BME-214524 can be incorporated into a student's educational journey in the college

According to the official course description,

"CDL matriculated students can use this course as part of their Educational Planning credit. As an educational planning study within the BME area, the course will be useful for BME students in any concentration; depending on the individual degree program design, it can be placed either as part of their concentration, or general learning. During the course, students will be required to present and evaluate concrete evidence of essential skills in all areas specified in the BME general guidelines; this activity is intended to strengthen the students' focus on learning outcomes of their college studies. This study can be taken at any point during the degree provided that prerequisite requirements are met. Students can discuss issues of timing with mentors. The advantage of taking it earlier (and before they finalize their degree plans) is that they should be better able to identify and understand their essential skills' gaps and then calibrate their ESC studies to address those deficiencies and build a stronger competency base. The advantage of taking it at a later stage is that they will have the opportunity to evaluate their progress and think proactively about their future self-improvement and career goals, including, but not limited to, graduate study".

Source: www.esc.edu

How BME-214524 can be incorporated into a business concentration (major)

This is an advance level business course dealing with an application of management, marketing, and business strategy to personal and professional development; as such, it further develops foundational concepts introduced in these courses. It is useful for senior undergraduate and graduate students specializing in any area of business, management and economics, as it helps better understand processes of self- and professional development and master practical skills, such as gathering evidence, conducting and making sense of self-assessment, and developing strategies for self-improvement and self-marketing. The course can be beneficial for managers and policy makers, as it is research based and can provide insights into recent trends in workforce development in a global context.

1.4. The use of E-portfolios

Why e-portfolio? What is an e-portfolio?

An evidence-based approach to self-management is concerned with collection of records of one's performance and their systematization, measurement, benchmarking, monitoring, etc. It is virtually impossible to conduct all these activities, organize and present their results without using a special instrument which can be a folder, a shelf, or a piece of software for organizing and storing digital copies. E-portfolio has become a popular tool to serve this purpose. These days e-portfolios are used for assessment, presentations, learning, personal development, etc. Elaine Danneler, Geoff Baker and Debra Henson [6, 7] developed an extensive bibliography and provide examples of how e-portfolios are used in educational settings similar to this course.

Read more about the use of e-portfolios[12]

Jon Mueller's authentic assessment toolbox[13]

The use of E-Portfolio and Learning Journal Workbook

In this course, we will be using a simplistic version of e-portfolio in the form of a single Word document. On the course webpage, you can find and download the E-Portfolio and Learning Journal Workbook Template. You will need to enter your personal information, rename the file and save it on your hard drive. It's a good idea to use your name in the file's name, for example <JoeDoeWorkbook.docx>. In each Module, there will be an e-portfolio task labelled EP1, EP2, etc. You'll be asked to continuously work in your Workbook and submit the entire Workbook in each Module. All e-portfolio submissions (in Modules 1-5) are subject to grading ; for each submission in Modules 1-5 you'll receive 2% of the course grade and in Module 6 you'll be required to review all entries and submit the Workbook as a final project (16% of the course grade). Overall, e-portfolio tasks (EP 1-5) and the final submission contribute 26% to your grade for the course. In some Modules, you'll be asked to use attachments (for example, your resume in Module 1, Professional Development Plan in Module 6, etc.).

---

[12] http://met.ubc.ca/program-overview/eportfolio-etec-590-graduating-project/
[13] http://jfmueller.faculty.noctrl.edu/toolbox/portfolios.htm

The optional use of Mahara

As a College student, you have access to Mahara, an e-portfolio system integrated with Moodle. The advantage of using Mahara is that you will have access to your e-portfolio across all courses and can possibly keep and use your material after you leave the college; the disadvantage is that it's less accessible for instructors and not convenient for grading and student-instructor communications. In addition, the way Mahara is structured is not consistent with the way we'll be using e-portfolio in this course. After careful considerations, we have decided to use a simplistic, text-based e-portfolio approach (not Mahara!) in this course. But you may want to create a version of your e-portfolio in Mahara and use it for your self-marketing presentation (Assignment 5).

The optional use of LinkedIn

LinkedIn (www.linkedin.com) is a popular social media tool; also, it can be used as an e-portfolio. We'll discuss the use of LinkedIn for your self-promotion in Module 5, but there is no requirement for you to actually use LinkedIn in this course.

Read more about using LinkedIn as a job search strategy[14].

1.5. Readings

1. Jackson, D. (2009). 'An international profile of industry-relevant competencies and skill gaps in modern graduates'. *International Journal of Management Education*, 8(3), 29-58. DOI:10.3794/jime.83.288. Available online at: http://www.heacademy.ac.uk/assets/bmaf/documents/publications/IJME/Vol8no3/3IJME288.pdf

2. Finch, D., Nadeau, J., and O'Reilly, N. The Future of Marketing Education: A Practitioner's Perspective. *Journal of Marketing Education. 2013, 35(1)*, 54-67. DOI: 10.1177/0273475312465091. Available online at: http://jmd.sagepub.com.library.esc.edu/content/35/1/54.full.pdf+html

3. DEST (2002). *Employability skills for the future: A report by the Australian Chamber of Commerce and Industry and the Business Council of Australia for the Department of Education, Science and Training*. Canberra, Australia. Available online at: http://hdl.voced.edu.au/10707/40939

4. Jackson, D. (2012). Business undergraduates' perceptions of their capabilities in employability skills: Implications for industry and higher education. *Industry and Higher Education, 26(5)*, 345-356. DOI: 10.5367/ihe.2012.0117. Available online at: http://ro.ecu.edu.au/cgi/viewcontent.cgi?article=1294&context=ecuworks2012&sei-redir=1&referer=http%3A%2F%2Fscholar.google.com.library.esc.edu%2Fscholar%3Fhl%3Den%26q%3Dbusiness%2Bundegraduates%2Bperceptions%2B2012%2BJackson%26btnG%3D%26as_sdt%3D1%252C33%26as_sdtp%3D#search=%22business%20undegraduates%20perceptions%202012%20Jackson%22

---

[14] http://www.cluteinstitute.com/ojs/index.php/AJBE/article/view/456/443

5. Bridgestock, R. (2009). "The graduate attributes we've overlooked: enhancing graduate employability through career management skills". *Higher Education Research and Development*, 28(1), 31-44. DOI: 10.1080/07294360802444347. Available online at: www.researchgate.net/publication/43206142_The_graduate_attributes_we%27ve_overlook ed__enhancing_graduate_employability_through_career_management_skills/file/50463520 6c490b35bc.pdf

6. Danneler, E. (2007). "The Portfolio approach to competency-based assessment at the Cleveland Clinic Lerner College of Medicine". *Academic Medicine, 82(5),* 493-502. Available online at: http://medicine.nova.edu/~danshaw/residents/readings/ThePortfolioApproachtoCompetenc y-BasedAssessment.pdf

7. Baker, G., and Henson, D. (2010). "Promoting employability skills development in a resear ch intensive university". *Education+Training*, 52(1), 62-75. DOI: http://dx.doi.org.library.e sc.edu/10.1108/00400911011017681. Available online at: http://search.proquest.com.librar y.esc.edu/docview/237074008?accountid=8067.

Module 2: Strategic Self-Analysis
Module 2 Overview

A thorough, meticulous, objective and honest self-analysis is the foundation of self-management. In Module 2 we introduce a comprehensive strategic approach to self-analysis designed for use in a business context. We begin with articles on theoretical foundations of self-analysis that are based on studies of personal attributes, such as individual thinking and learning styles, conducted by cognitive, educational and organizational psychologists. This group of researchers demonstrated that in order to strategically plan and perform self-developmental activities individuals must develop specific, metacognitive and self-regulatory skills and motivational beliefs. When empowered with those skills and beliefs, individuals become self-directed, strategically oriented and more efficient in performing various activities, such as education (self-directed learners) and work (goal-oriented employees). In the following chapter, we examine the specifics of self-analysis in a competitive business environment. In particular, we'll see that in a competitive job market where individuals compete for jobs/promotions and are routinely benchmarked against standards, best practices and each other's performances, it is critically important for an employee/job seeker to develop an objective, external view of her/his own competencies and skills. Taking an external perspective is helpful for conducting an objective, evidence-based self-assessment, correctly interpreting its results by comparing and rating them against standards or the competition, and then developing sound strategies for self-promotion and self-development. In this chapter we review analytical methods and tools including benchmarking that were originally developed by business strategists for organizations striving to achieve competitive advantage and discuss whether and how some of those methods and tools can be used by individuals aiming to succeed in a competitive job market. In the end, we describe a model of strategic self-analysis as the cornerstone of self-management in a competitive business environment.

Learning activities are based on the Module's readings and designed to engage you in strategic self-analysis. In the beginning, each student is asked to identify her/his professional and generic skills (E-portfolio task EP2). For the duration of the Module students are required to participate in Discussion 2 on the use of strategic business models for personal development. As a culminating activity, each student is required to come up with a description of a real or fictional position and prepare a skills analysis responding to specified selection criteria (Written Assignment 2). In the most part the selection criteria are based on the SUNY ESC's requirements for students in the BME area. The first learning goal of Written Assignment 2 is to connect this course with degree planning activities previously undertaken by the students and examine how studies included into the degree program can be useful for developing skills required in "real life". Another learning goal is to demonstrate that curricular mapping is a necessary, but not sufficient step in students' preparation; the fact that a student has taken a particular course doesn't necessarily guarantee that the student has obtained and can demonstrate evidence of mastery in performing a certain skill at the required level. Yet another and the main learning goal of this exercise is to help students develop an objective, external view of their skills/capabilities as a prerequisite for strategic self-analysis and self-assessment.

Learning Objectives of Module 2 are the following:

- Get familiar with psychological theories dealing with self-awareness, personal traits and qualities, thinking and learning styles; review and discuss the concepts of self-regulation, metacognition, motivation, and self-directedness in relation to self-analysis and self-development;

- Examine the specifics of self-analysis in a competitive business environment; review main ideas and some instruments of strategic business analysis and discuss their relevance for self-analysis and self-development;

- Identify your goals, professional skills and generic skills;

- Acting in a simulated, similar to a real life setting (a competitive job search) demonstrate how you can conduct a brief self-analysis and respond to a job advertising by crafting a detailed selection criteria statement.

Learning Activities include:

- Readings (this content guide and suggested additional sources);

- Discussion D2;

- E-Portfolio task EP2;

- Written Assignment A2.

Schedule and due dates (see Course Information Document).

2.1. Theoretical Foundations of Self-Analysis

Self-awareness

Engaging in self-observation and developing self-awareness is the first step of self-management. In any large book store, as well as online, you can find many scholarly, as well as popular, "know thyself" type of sources dealing with problems of understanding of the self and others, explaining and exploring topics like human life cycles, body and wellness, mind and mind power, thinking skills and creativity, behavior styles, spirit and self-esteem, values and interests, lifelong learning, work and life balance, and personal life strategies. As a short cut, you may find it useful to conduct a brief google search and get familiar with the concept of self-awareness (an example[15]).

If you are interested to learn more about how "knowing thyself" translates into job readiness, you may find it useful to conduct a personality assessment test using the Holland's hexagon model[16]. A renowned career theorist, Holland developed a model of six personality types (Realistic, Conventional, Enterprising, Social, Artistic, and Investigative) where typical careers match certain personality types. These days many career centers use this model (see an example[17]) to help students find out about their personality type and possible careers/occupations they are supposed to be leaning to according to Holland.

More resources on self-analysis[18].

A brief resource guide on talent management

Sometimes people are not very much interested in knowing more about themselves as employees, but their employers typically do want to know about ways to increase productivity of their human capital. A selection of employee testing tools can be found on the Pan's Powered website (www.panpowered.com). Using this search tool, you can find companies specializing in development of assessment and self-assessment tools for employers and learn about their products. For example, "My Thinking Styles" assessment developed by Judy Chartrand for THINK Watson[19] is administered by Pearson (a sample report is freely available online[20]). According to the author, identifying a person's thinking style can help the person become more aware of how she/he approaches problems and opportunities, evaluates information, makes decisions, and takes actions. As a result, the person is supposed to become more aware of her/his strengths and how to use them on the job. Another popular tools for finding personal strengths are offered by Gallup (StrengthsFinder[21]) and Hogan[22]. Yet another set of assessment tools is developed by TalentLens (talentlens.com). On their website you can find sample reports demonstrating how they approach skills assessment, the range of assessable skills and the way achieved scores are interpreted.

On individual differences and learning styles

When conducting self-analysis, it's helpful to know about one's thinking and learning styles. The concepts of styles ("thinking style", "learning style") are widely used by psychologists to capture individual differences and explain how people within categories think, learn and approach problems. If this is something that truly interests you, you may want it useful to take at some point a formal class in educational psychology or read a textbook on that subject. For the purpose

---

[15] http://psychology.about.com/od/cognitivepsychology/fl/What-Is-Self-Awareness.htm
[16] http://www.hollandcodes.com/holland_code_career.html
[17] http://www.explorecareersandcollegemajors.com/holland_codes.html
[18] http://emergentbydesign.com/2011/11/03/8-tools-for-self-analysis-mapping-your-strengths-gifts-roles/
[19] http://www.thinkwatson.com/mythinkingstyles
[20] http://www.thinkwatson.com/downloads/MyThinkingStyles-SampleReport.pdf
[21] http://strengths.gallup.com/110440/About-StrengthsFinder-2.aspx
[22] http://www.hoganassessments.com/content/we-predict-performance

of this class, we recommend that you read excerpts from three articles. When reading, try to identify your own learning style and think about how you can use a better understanding of your personality type when looking for a job.

Mark Morrison, Arthur Sweeney and Troy Heffenan ("Learning Styles of On-Campus and Off- Campus Marketing Students: The Challenge for Marketing Educators", *Journal of Marketing Education*, 2003, vol. 25(3), pp. 208-217) provide a brief introduction to theories of learning styles (pp. 209-210), particularly the one of Solomon-Felder and their Index of Learning Styles that includes four dimensions (active/reflective, visual/verbal, sensing/intuitive and sequential/global). Knowing a person's learning style helps better understand the person's teaching and learning preferences and even job potential (p. 215).

David Ackerman and Jing Hu ("Effect of Type of Curriculum on Educational Outcomes and Motivation among Marketing Students with Different Learning Styles", *Journal of Marketing Education*, 2011, Vol. 33(3), pp. 273-284) describe Kolb's Learning Style Inventory, Dunn and Dunn's model of learning style preferences, and use Martinez's model of learning orientation where learning styles can be categorized into four groups: transforming learners, performing learners, conforming learners and resistance learners (pp. 273-275). The authors' conclusion is that autonomous learners benefit from hands-on projects, cases and simulations; less autonomous learners are less willing to take the initiative or responsibility for their learning.

Hulia Julie Yazici ("A study of collaborative learning style and team learning performance. *Education & Training*, 2005, 47(2), pp. 216-229) uses another model, the Grasha-Riechmann Student Learning Style Scale (GRSLSS), to assess the learning style preferences of business students enrolled in an operations management class. GRSLSS measures learning styles as personal qualities that influence a student's ability to acquire information, to interact with peers and the teacher, and otherwise to participate in learning experiences. According to the authors,

"The learning styles inventory promotes understanding of learning in a broad context, spanning six categories: competitive, collaborative, avoidant, participant, dependent, and independent. Competitive students learn material in order to perform better than others in the class. Collaborative students feel they can learn by sharing ideas and talents. Avoidant style learners are not enthusiastic about learning content and attending class. Participants are good citizens in class. They are eager to do as much of the required and optional course requirements. Dependent learners show little intellectual curiosity and they learn only what is required. They view teacher and peers as sources of structure and support and look for authority figures. Independent learners like to think for themselves and are confident in their learning abilities: they prefer to learn the content that they feel is important" (p. 222).

Self-control, self-regulation, metacognition and motivation

Self-control, or an ability to engage in self-observation, planning, goal setting, organizing, self-monitoring and self-evaluation, is the quintessence of self-management. In recent years, the concept of self-control has been actively researched in its application to the field of education; this research area has become known as self-regulated learning (SRL). To get familiar with its main ideas, we highly recommend you reading an article by Barry Zimmerman on the topic

("Self-regulated learning and academic achievement: an overview". *Educational Psychologist*, 1990, 25(1), 3-17) or a more recent work by Traci Sitzmann and Katherine Ely ("Meta-Analysis of Self-Regulated Learning in Work-Related Training and Educational Attainment: What We Know and Where We Need to Go". *Psychological Bulletin*, 2011, 137 (3), 421–442).

In a nutshell, SRL is about 'learning to learn' and then using this crucial skill for self-improvement. There are several aspects of SRL including metacognition, motivation and behavior. Metacognition deals with understanding of one's thinking and learning processes; it enables self-awareness and manifests in a meaningful and efficient planning, goal setting, and self-monitoring. In terms of motivation, self-regulated learners develop and maintain interest, demonstrate high persistence and self-efficacy. Behaviorally, they create personal learning environments, actively seek feedback and develop capabilities for self-instruction.

Self-directedness and strategic approach to self-management

Self-directedness is a practical application of self-regulation. Broadly speaking, self-directed are those individuals that take full responsibility for all or most aspects of their life. In a narrow sense, self-directedness applies to learning. Self-directed learning (SDL) is a strategic process where individuals analyze their learning needs, formulate learning goals, identify resources, choose and implement strategies and evaluate learning outcomes. A good introduction to SDL can be found in an article by Andrea Ellinger (The Concept of Self-Directed Learning and Its Implications for Human Resource Development, in *Advances in Developing Human Resources*, May 2004, vol. 6, no. 2, pp. 158-177).

The concept of self-directedness is very useful to understand how self-management works. To be self-directed, an individual must learn how to effectively control her/his own self and make sure that daily routines contribute to fulfillment of established goals. A toolbox of required skills includes self-observation, self-analysis, goal setting, perseverance and self-regulation, self-monitoring and self-assessment. To efficiently observe and monitor oneself, one needs to develop reflective skills. This is the heart and soul of self-management.

Reflection and the role of learning journals

When managing others, a manager needs to establish and maintain a system of records describing tasks and helping monitor performance. Similarly, self-management is easier when there is a written record of self-observation. A discussion of benefits of reflecting practice and various approaches to journaling can be found here[23]. In this course, we will use a single document combining a reflective journal and an e-portfolio.

---

[23] http://www.tru.ca/__shared/assets/reflective_learner19767.pdf

2.2. Conducting Self-Analysis in a Business Context

What difference does the context make?

In the previous chapter, we described theoretical foundations of self-analysis and introduced concepts of self-regulation and self-directedness. In this chapter, we examine the specifics of self-analysis in a business context. Then, in the following chapter, we describe a model of strategic self-analysis as the cornerstone of self-management in a competitive business environment.

In a competitive job market individuals compete for jobs/promotions and are routinely benchmarked against standards, best practices and each other's performances. If someone wants to learn a particular skill to increase her/his employability, this individual must develop a fairly good idea about the required level of performance to withstand the competition. Therefore, when conducting self-analysis in a business context, an individual must be aware of desired skills/levels of competency, her/his factual skills/levels of competency and develop an objective, external view of her/his own performance. Taking an external perspective is helpful for conducting an objective, evidence-based self-analysis and self-assessment, correctly interpreting its results by comparing and rating them against standards or the competition, and then developing sound strategies for self-development.

Benchmarking

Benchmarking is the key component of self-analysis in a business context; to find out about true strengths and weaknesses in someone's' skill repertoire, it should be compared and matched with the competition. Contemporary learning theories are not concerned with this problem; not surprisingly that the training and development literature dealing with self-developmental issues actively borrow ideas and approaches from the business strategy literature where the concept of competitive benchmarking was born. That's how "personal SWOT", "personal balanced scoring card" and the like models have been introduced for developmental purposes.

In this module, we review analytical methods and tools including benchmarking that were originally developed by business strategists for organizations striving to achieve competitive advantage and discuss whether and how some of those methods and tools can be used by individuals aiming to succeed in a competitive job market. To begin with, we review main ideas of business strategy and discuss whether and if yes then how it can be used for strategic self-management.

A "crash" course on strategy

It is likely that as a business student you are already familiar with the concept of business strategy and have mastered some tools of strategic planning. In preparation for this Module's activities, you may find it useful to browse your old textbooks or google <business strategy> and review search results. To make sure that we are on the same page, we would like to take a minute and improvise a "crash course" on strategy.

In its simplest definition, **strategy** is about going from here to there where "here" is the current and "there" a desired situation in a competitive and ever changing environment. Strategic approach typically requires a strategist to begin with conducting an analysis where s/he would identify values and goals of the organization and its main stakeholders, then analyses external and internal environments and future trends, conducts internal analysis and benchmarks the organization against its competition, examines the current and formulates a range of possible future strategies, recommends one of those and suggests implementation steps and control strategies. In ancient times, strategic approach was widely used by military and political leaders; in the modern era strategy was re-invented and is commonly used by large corporations, non-profit and governmental bodies and even small businesses. Strategic models and tools can also be used by individuals.

Developing business strategy is not a science, but a way of disciplined thinking; as such, it is helpful for analyzing the environment, identifying available choices, developing a logical course of actions. As a result, strategic thinking may yield significant benefits. It is believed that if a business, organization or an individual has done the analytical part right and is capable of pursuing a coordinated course of actions, chances are that it will indeed be possible to get from "here" to "there" or at least very close. But how can an individual engage in strategic planning? Are there any rules or "scientific" recommendations?

Of course, there are no "magic" tools and the fact that someone uses "scientific" methods like SWOT analysis provides no guarantee. When conducting strategic analysis, it is important to understand its logic and the way business strategists use their instruments to obtain meaningful results. Having said that, let's examine what some of the popular concepts/instruments of strategic analysis are and how they can be used for self-analysis.

Strategy: In the beginning, it should be very clearly and explicitly stated where you are going from and where you want to be.

Mission/vision: This is a very crucial point for strategic analysis. For a company, typical questions are: Who are we? What business are we in? What do we want to be? In 1 year? In 5 years from now? Similar questions should be asked by an individual conducting strategic self-analysis.

Stakeholders: Who are significant others? What is their influence? How might this affect your plans? There are specific tools to analyze stakeholders and their influence, but it's probably better not to dig too deep at this stage.

External scanning: What is the external environment and its boundaries? What is happening in the environment politically? Economically? Socially? Culturally? Technologically? Why does (or doesn't) it matter in your case? What opportunities and threats are present in the external environment? Today and in near future?

Competitive environment: What is the immediate competition in attaining your goal(s)? What are the key success factors typically shared by successful competitors and apparently required in this particular environment to succeed? What else is happening in this industry (occupation, location)? Short term and long term trends? What opportunities and threats are in the internal (competitive) environment?

Internal analysis and benchmarking: What are your capabilities, attitudes and dispositions, competencies and skills? Are your knowledge base and preparation sufficient? What are your chances to succeed in the competitive environment, now and in the future?

Summary: Strategic summary combines the results of external and internal analyses and provides a foundation for strategy formulation.

Strategy formulation begins with identification and evaluation of alternatives. Oftentimes it requires **making assumptions** about changes in the environment and competitive moves and re-evaluating previous analyses. Strategy making is not a one-time process!

Once the overall strategy is formulated and translated into a series of steps and **functional strategies**, it should be consistently **implemented, monitored and controlled**.

Strategic tools

There are many strategic models that are commonly used to conduct analyses and present findings. One of the most popular is SWOT (Strengths, Weaknesses, Opportunities, Threats).

SWOT is a model (=strategic tool) to present a summary of findings where Opportunities and Threats identified by scanning external and internal environments are matched against internal Weaknesses and Strengths. This tool is developed to summarize findings of strategic analysis, evaluate current and formulate new strategies. SWOT is a popular tool that is often used, but also commonly misunderstood. To properly use SWOT analysis one needs to meticulously conduct all required analytical procedures.

A typical mistake, for example, is to start working on strategic analysis by doing SWOT. Without developing a reasonably good understanding of the environment and ongoing trends it is very easy to miscalculate opportunities, threats, strengths and weaknesses. Let's consider a hypothetical situation where someone is an exceptionally good typist and sees it as a major strength to build a job search strategy. This person might be upset to find out that due to advances in speech recognition technology typing speed may no longer be seen by employers as an advantage.

Another typical mistake is to mix up an external threat and an internal weakness ("my weakness is that my skill has no value any more"). You cannot change the environment; it is beyond your control, so some changes in the external environment can present a threat if you are not prepared to change internally. The question is whether you can see that your real weakness is perhaps your inability to scan the environment and change. If you engage in scanning the environment and will be looking for ways to adapt and succeed, it is likely that you will soon identify a new set of skills to develop and won't be concentrating on your outdated skill.

Another, less known tool is called VRINE (Valuable, Rare, Inimitable, Non-substitutable, Exploitable) and designed for benchmarking resources and capabilities of competing firms. More on SWOT analysis[24].

---

[24] http://www.mindtools.com/pages/article/newTMC_05.htm

<u>Using business strategy for personal development</u>

In organizations, some people (like CEO) do strategic planning on a full time basis; this is their job. Is there any sense for an average person to engage in strategic self-planning? Even if the answer is affirmative, does personal strategy making need to be that elaborated and multistage as the corporate one? Are there any shortcuts? Actually, this is a very interesting question and we would like to leave it for discussion D2. To begin with, you may google <personal SWOT analysis>. Here is an <u>example</u>[25].

2.3. Self-Analysis for Competitive Advantage

<u>What we've got so far</u>

Building on the advances in cognitive psychology, we concluded that self-management was based upon metacognitive, self-regulatory and motivational processes that allow individuals to develop capabilities for self-observation, self-awareness, self-analysis, goal setting, self-programming, self-monitoring and self-directing. Self-regulatory techniques and approaches include self-observation, self-reflection, self-monitoring and journaling, self-analysis and self-assessment, feedback and support seeking, and strategic, long term orientation. When functioning in a business context and using self-management for achieving competitive advantage on the job market, an individual must be acutely aware of required skills/levels of competency, set her/his learning goals accordingly, develop an objective, external view of her/his own performance and establish an effective process for strategic self-analysis and self-assessment based on benchmarking of her/his performance against relevant standards, best practices in the field or the competition. While psychological theories allow us to understand the foundations and internal mechanics of self-management, we need specific, operational approaches and tools for implementing self-management in a business context. Some of the approaches and tools can be borrowed from strategic management including strategic analysis of external environments, identification of key success factors, competitive benchmarking, and SWOT analysis.

<u>A model for strategic self-analysis in a business context</u>

Below is an outline of the model for strategic self-analysis designed for use in a business context that we'll be using in this course. It begins with Stage 1 by establishing an internally oriented system and a process for self-observation, self-monitoring and self-reflection. To do so, students are required to set up a learning journal and an e-portfolio (learning activities EP-1, EP-2, A1). Then, it continues with Stage 2 by conducting an analysis of the external environment (job market) and identifying a position (or, a range of positions) of interest and specifying required competencies, skills and levels of performance (learning activity A2). Stages 3-5 deal with three stages of internal analysis: collecting evidence of performance (step 3, learning activities EP-3 and A3), collecting materials for benchmarking and conducting self-assessment (Stage 4, learning activities EP-3 and A3) and making sense of results and findings (Stage 5, learning activities EP-4 and A4). Stage 6 is concerned with formulation and implementation of personal

---

self-developmental strategies that are built on strategic self-analysis (learning activities EP-4 and A4). Stage 7 deals with some functional strategies, including self-marketing and self-promotion, feedback seeking and ongoing professional development (learning activities EP-5 and A5). Stage 8 closes the loop (learning activities A6, EP-6 and final submission of the Workbook).

Stages	Description	Tools used	Activities
Stage 1. Self-observation. Self-monitoring. Self-reflection	Establish an internally-oriented system and a process for self-observation, self-monitoring and self-reflection	Learning Journal E-portfolio	EP-1, EP-2, A1
Stage 2. External analysis and goal setting	Identify critical skills areas and performance indicators (key success factors for competitive advantage in the chosen field)	Learning journal, external resources	A2
Stage 3. Internal analysis I	Create a personal self-development lab. Collect evidence of own performance in the specified skills areas	E-portfolio,	EP-3, A3
Stage 4. Internal analysis II	Collect evidence of best practices, standards in the specified skills areas. Select tools for self-assessment. Conduct self-assessment by benchmarking your performance against standards or competition	E-portfolio. Rubrics, checklists, self-assessment tool	EP-3, A3
Stage 5. Internal analysis III	Organize and make sense of findings. Identify strengths and weaknesses, opportunities and threats	Dashboard, SWOT	EP-4, A4
Stage 6. Strategy formulation and implementation	Formulate self-developmental strategy building on strengths, eliminating weaknesses. Develop a process for self-monitoring, motivating and reinforcing the strategy (self-programming)	Balanced scoring card	EP-4, A4
Stage 7. External view, self-marketing and self-promotion	Establish an externally-oriented system for presenting your skills and a strategy for self-marketing and self-promotion. Solicit developmental feedback. Make sure that your self-assessment is accurate	E-portfolio Website, Blog, PPT	EP-5, A5
Stage 8. Closing the loop	Continue developing as a self-directed learner; use and refine your strategic self-analytical skills; review and if needed revise your goals	Learning journal, self-development plan	EP-6, FP, A6

A personal self-development lab

To efficiently use the described above model, one needs to engage in collecting evidence of own performance in the specified skills areas, collecting evidence of best practices and standards in the specified skills areas, selecting tools for self-assessment, conducting self-assessment by benchmarking her/his performance against standards or competition, and organizing and making sense of findings. This is what we call a personal lab for self-development.

Next steps explained (Assignment 2 and beyond)

All students participating in this course are uniquely positioned in their external environment; therefore, critical skills areas for positions (jobs) they may want to get are different. Particularly, required professional skills can be very distinctive. In order to be on the same page with the entire class, we chose to concentrate on generic, transferrable skills. In Assignment 2 students are required to conduct an analysis of their respective external environments and come up with a description for a real of fictional position that is of interest to them. Most importantly, students have to describe key selection criteria for potential candidates for this position emphasizing required competencies and skills for that position. This is a very important assignment as each student will be constantly referring to the selection criteria s/he specified for the duration of the course.

It is up to students how they may approach external analysis; each industry, region or company is unique. Also, students may choose to think about a position that is in close proximity or "think big" about a dream job. It may be helpful to use business strategy tools like PEST analysis[26] to identify future trends and prospects for each occupation or use the Occupational Outlook Handbook[27] published by the U.S. Department of Labor.

Once you will have identified critical skills areas and performance indicators (key success factors for competitive advantage in the chosen field), you'll be ready to engage in internal (self) analysis and self-assessment which is the subject matter of the next two modules.

2.4. Readings

1. Morrison, M., Sweeney, A., and Heffenan, T. (2003). "Learning Styles of On-Campus and Off-Campus Marketing Students: The Challenge for Marketing Educators", *Journal of Marketing Education*, 2003, 25(3), 208-217. DOI: 10.1177/0273475303257520. Available online at: http://jmd.sagepub.com.library.esc.edu/content/25/3/208.short
2. Ackerman, D., and Jing Hu (2011). "Effect of Type of Curriculum on Educational Outcomes and Motivation among Marketing Students with Different Learning Styles", *Journal of Marketing Education*, 33(3), 273-284. DOI: 10.1177/0273475311420233. Available online at: http://jmd.sagepub.com.library.esc.edu/content/33/3/273.short
3. Yazici, H. J. (2005). A study of collaborative learning style and team learning performance. *Education & Training*, 47(2), 216-229. Available online at: http://search.proquest.com.library.esc.edu/docview/237070712/fulltextPDF?accountid=8067
4. Sitzmann, T., and Ely, K. (2011). Meta-Analysis of Self-Regulated Learning in Work-Related Training and Educational Attainment: What We Know and Where We Need to Go. *Psychological Bulletin*, 137(3), 421–442. Available online at: http://eds.b.ebscohost.com.library.esc.edu/ehost/pdfviewer/pdfviewer?sid=3e8bb1fe-f86c-4f04-9365-2550a2e671d7%40sessionmgr113&vid=1&hid=116. Accessed July 31, 2014.
5. Zimmerman, B. J. (1990). "Self-Regulated Learning and Academic Achievement: An Overview". *Educational Psychologist*, 25(1), 3-17. DOI: 10.1207/s15326985ep2501_2. Available online at: http://eds.b.ebscohost.com.library.esc.edu/ehost/pdfviewer/pdfviewer?sid=6536dbef-f61f-4631-b62c-d6788b80b63f%40sessionmgr110&vid=1&hid=116 Accessed July 31, 2014.
6. Ellinger, A. (2004). The Concept of Self-Directed Learning and Its Implications for Human Resource Development. *Advances in Developing Human Resources, 6(2)*, 158-177. DOI: 10.1177/1523422304263327. Available online at: http://adh.sagepub.com.library.esc.edu/content/6/2/158.short. Accessed August 4, 2014.

---

[26] http://www.mindtools.com/pages/article/newTMC_09.htm
[27] http://www.bls.gov/ooh/

Module 3: Self-Assessment
Module 3 Overview

Module 3 deals with self-assessment. In order to conduct a thorough and objective self-assessment, it is critically important to approach it from an external point of view. That's why we begin with a brief overview of a typical selection process and then ask you to review your own skills analysis crafted in Module 2 Assignment 2 by looking through the lens of a prospective employer and reflecting on it in Discussion 3. Then, we discuss foundations and mechanics of self-assessment drawing from four distinctly different bodies of literature (educational psychology, vocational development and training, graduate employability skills and management science). In particular, we review self-assessment principles as formulated by educational theorists and practitioners, examine assessment and self-assessment methodologies, frameworks, instruments and tools, review the use of self-assessment techniques in relation to transition from college to work and the formation of graduate employability skills, observe approaches to collecting, organizing, presenting and evaluating evidence and explain the approach to self-assessment taken in this course. In conclusion, we examine how business strategists approach self-assessment and discuss whether some of the business strategy tools (like VRINE model) or their modifications can be used for personal self-assessment. To integrate various approaches to self-assessment we suggest that you engage into a discussion on the use of a personal VRINE analysis (Discussion D3). This discussion is designed to help you identify your critical professional and generic skills areas, subareas and elements of competency and come up with approaches to "pinpoint", collect evidence of your performance and benchmark it against standards or best practices in the field (also, see E-portfolio Task EP3). As a practical application, students will be able to download and use a special instrument developed for this course ("Self-Assessment Tool"). The goal of Written Assignment 3 is to describe the process of self-assessment and reflect on the suggested readings.

Learning Objectives of Module **3** are the following:

- Examine a typical job selection process and develop an objective, critical ("outside") perspective for self-assessment;

- Examine educational theories dealing with self-assessment; review approaches to collecting, organizing and presenting evidence presented in the literature on vocational education and training; discuss assessment and self-assessment instruments and tools in the graduate employability literature;

- Review main ideas, approaches and instruments of strategic business analysis in relation to assessment and self-assessment and discuss their use for personal self-assessment;

- Practice self-assessment with the use of Self-Assessment Tool.

Learning Activities include:

- Readings (this content guide and suggested additional sources);

- Discussion D3;

- E-Portfolio task EP3;

- Written Assignment A3.

Schedule and due dates (see Course Information Document).

3.1. From external assessment to self-assessment

In Module 2, you were asked to specify a job description and a list of selection criteria and prepare a skills analysis by crafting a selection criteria statement and elaborating on your professional and generic capabilities, competencies and skills. Now, it is time to review and discuss your application. Most importantly, how will a prospective employer read and evaluate it? To begin with, it seems to be a good idea to think about how the selection process usually works. You may want to get some additional information by browsing specialized websites (example[28]) and by googling <employee selection>.

From the employer's perspective, an employee selection process normally starts with the needs analysis and crafting a job advertising message where key competencies, skills, and experiences of a prospective employee are emphasized. As selection is typically a highly competitive process, key selection criteria are usually explicitly formulated to allow candidates prepare and submit an informative application package. Then, selection officers (or selection committee members) use scoring sheets to assign rankings to applicants' statements and credentials; if all selection criteria are met by a number of applicants, ranking helps choosing those candidates who seem to better fit for the job and can get through the initial screening for a face-to-face interview. After that, the selection process continues with presentations, interviews, demonstrations by invited candidates to select the best candidate for the job; those events are usually attended and assessed by designated officers (committee members). Overall, it's all about revealing and comparing pieces of the candidates' evidence of mastery in performing required skills.[29]

For a candidate, a clear understanding of how selection process works can be very helpful in their job search and preparation. From a practical perspective, an ability "to put yourself in their shoes", i.e., seeing her/his application through the lens of a prospective employer, with a list of selection criteria and a ranking sheet in mind, is itself a valuable skill to complement job-seeking strategies. At the same time, an ability to develop an objective and critical ("outside") view of oneself adds up to self-awareness, self-analysis and self-management. By developing an external perspective, the candidate will learn how to see her/his unique combination of knowledge and skills in a competitive environment where all capabilities and their combination have to be

---

[28] http://smallbusiness.chron.com/employee-selection-process-2568.html

[29] See more in the Assessment Decision Guide developed by the U.S. Office of Personnel Management available online at http://www.opm.gov/policy-data-oversight/assessment-and-selection/reference-materials/assessmentdecisionguide.pdf

pinpointed, demonstrated, proved, benchmarked, and rated. Also, the use of an outside, objective perspective validates self- assessment and ensures the integrity of the process. That's why in the reminder of this course we suggest that you "internalize" a selection committee member's external view of yourself and from that objective perspective critically review and thoroughly examine your own capabilities, knowledge and skills base, and performance.

Now, with this external perspective in mind, we suggest that you act as a prospective employer and engage in reviewing your own skills analysis. As the employer, you are supposed to know very well about the most important skills that are required for the position (let's use the term Critical Skills Areas, or CSA). How would you approach the process of assessment? It seems logical to look for CSAs in the application; then, collect, observe and assess evidence of the candidate's preparation and performance using a ranking sheet. To do so, you will need a collection of assessment tools and some kind of methodology and experience in using the tools. As a result, you'll be able to gather and organize evidence, conduct a thorough investigation and come up with a meaningful, objective conclusion.

In Discussion D3 you are asked to reflect on your skills analysis A2 by taking an employer's point of view. How would you rate your own application? What are your chances to get the job? Why? How can you make yourself the best candidate? How could you improve your job application? How can it inform your self-analysis?

3.2. How to approach self-assessment

Taking an external ("an employer's") perspective provides with a valid objective approach to self-analysis and self-assessment in a competitive environment. As in the previous part on self-analysis, we'll be drawing from different streams of literature. In the educational psychology and vocational training literature we can find well-developed approaches to gathering and organizing evidence and conducting self-assessment with the use of special tools (rubrics, checklists, observations, etc.). In the business strategy literature we can find approaches to self-assessment designed for use in a competitive environment.

Self-assessment as a student's self-developmental strategy

A central role self-assessment plays in developing self-developmental strategies is emphasized by Georgina Loacker of Alverno College when she quoted one of her students saying that '*You have to be able to have an accurate idea of where you are and how you are doing...It's very difficult...unless you are able to figure out how it is that you are doing and that takes practice to get accurate and realistic*' [1]. In the same article, she defined self-assessment as "*not merely a matter of self-grading, nor an occasional summative analysis of a series of one's performances. It is an ongoing process of evaluating one's performance in a way that makes it sustained and sustaining essential part of lifelong learning*". According to G. Loacker [1], seven concepts of self-assessment include the following:

- The understanding and practice of self-assessment as a developmental process where initially a beginning student expects someone else (typically, the teacher) to take the initiative in recognizing problems and pointing out concrete evidence to the student to make judgments on her behavior/performance. Understanding of self-assessment increases with practice; typically, it takes a few years of consistent practice in self-assessment for a student to internalize standards of self-assessment.

- A second concept is the use of observable performance as the basis or evidence for judgment. It is particularly important for students to discern patterns of strengths and weaknesses that can assist them in their plans for improvement.

- The third concept deals with careful observation. The challenge of precise observation lies especially in the ability to separate one's self from actual performance. For this reason it is important to assist a student to understand that each self-assessment is an evaluation, not of the person, but of a performance in a specific context or a series of performances in various contexts. The self is doing the judging as the agent rather than being judged as the object.

- For an understanding of one's observations, the fourth concept, a reflection, plays an essential role. Getting at the how and why of one's actions seems to be an obvious step to avoid leaping to judgment.

- A fifth concept incorporated into self-assessment as a developing process is that of the use of criteria that are gradually internalized. A given student might know that effective organization is a criterion for good writing, but it takes some time to understand exactly what that means in performance, how context and audience require it to vary, and how one integrates its myriad nuances and varieties and levels of expression.

- The development of criteria is enhanced by instructor and peer feedback, which is the sixth defining concept identified here as essential to the kind of self-assessment needed for lifelong learning. Through such feedback, a student expands his or her operational understanding of what constitutes effective performance. Feedback from instructors and peers can highlight points the student missed, can discover gaps in the student's analysis, can provide other perspectives from which to view a performance, and can raise questions that might lead to further understanding.

- The final concept is planning for improvement. Clearly the process of careful observation and reflective judgment, if recorded, can provide valuable information for ongoing improvement. Specifically, it can assist students to transform vague hopes into realistic goal setting. A goal might be set for the next single performance until it becomes a habit or it might span a semester or year. In any case, it encourages the student to reexamine and verify his or her intuitive decisions as well as intentionally informed ones.

Issues of reliability, validity, and utility of self-assessment are discussed by John Ross in his article published by Practical Assessment, Research and Evaluation in 2006.

Self-assessment in a vocational setting

Vocational education and training is concerned with skills acquisition and assessment and thus can provide with well-developed approaches to self-assessment including methodologies, frameworks and tools. A good example is presented by "Innovation and Business Skills Australia" which is one of several councils designated by the Australian government for assessing vocational skills (http://www.ibsa.org.au). According to that approach, skills can be formally assessed and recognized as qualifications where a so called **unit of competency** is the smallest unit that can be assessed and recognized. Units of competency are comprised of **elements of competency;** elements describe the essential outcomes of a unit of competency. For each element of competency, there are **performance criteria** and an **evidence guide**.

The described vocational approach can be very useful for self-assessment, as it provides with a well-developed framework and describes assessment methods and instruments. For example, the competency unit TAEASS502A[30] *'Design and develop assessment tools'* consists of four elements of competency (determine focus of the assessment tool; design assessment tool; develop assessment tool and review and trial assessment tool). Each element of competency has 3-5 performance criteria; for example, the element *'Determine focus of the assessment tool'* has the following performance criteria: a) identify target group of candidates, purposes of assessment tool, and contexts in which the tool will be used; b) access relevant benchmarks for assessment and interpret them to establish evidence required to demonstrate competence; c) identify, access and interpret organizational, legal and ethical requirements for relevant contextualization guidelines; d) identify other related documentation to inform assessment for self-development. For all elements of competency, required basic skills and knowledge are identified. The evidence guide provides advice on assessment, a range of appropriate assessment methods, techniques and instruments. In another document developed by IBSA[31] there is a substantial list of more than 30 assessment methods and tools, including a description of each method and tool and suggestions about when to use them; many of the tools are applicable for self-assessment. A more detailed guide on developing assessment tools, including self-assessment, in a vocational setting is provided by the National Quality Council[32].

Self-assessment for professional development

For the sake of brevity, professional development trainers oftentimes come up with a list of key skills/competencies comprised of elements of competency, and suggest a simplified tool for self-assessment. One example[33] is presented by Exeter University in UK. Another example[34] is developed by Rich Young for professionals in the field of business communications.

---

[30] https://training.gov.au/TrainingComponentFiles/TAE10/TAEASS502A_R1.pdf
[31] https://www.google.com/url?sa=t&rct=j&q=&esrc=s&source=web&cd=3&ved=0CC0QFjAC&url=https%3A%2F%2Fwww.ibsa.org.au%2Fsites%2Fdefault%2Ffiles%2Fmedia%2FTAEASS401B%2520PW%2520APPENDIX%25202.docx&ei=3yniU5jgK4yMyATTjIDgAg&usg=AFQjCNEw5KfLuNH31MY-FSSKfYAadsYCTQ&bvm=bv.72197243,d.aWw&cad=rja
[32] http://www.nssc.natese.gov.au/__data/assets/pdf_file/0011/51023/Validation_and_Moderation_-_Guide_for_developing_assessment_tools.pdf
[33] https://www.exeter.ac.uk/media/level1/academicserviceswebsite/studentandstaffdevelopment/documents/pdp/Personal_and_Key_Skills_Self_Assessment_Audit.pdf

3.3. Assessment/self-assessment methods and tools

Which tools are available?

In the above referenced document by IBSA the authors mention a range of **assessment methods**, including observation in workplace, observation in simulated work environment, fault finding, role-playing, construction of role-play, games, game construction, verbal questioning, verbal presentation to assessor, verbal presentation to assessor and audience, formal oral examination, oral examination with panel, interview, debate, production of audio/ visual and other multimedia application, production of slide tape series, production of audio, group discussion, formal examination, short-answer test, take home examination, open book test or examination, multiple-choice answer test, essay, free choice essay, project (can also include a work-based project), documents, third party reports, training records, portfolio. While most of these methods require that an assessor (or a group of assessors and peer-reviewers) is involved, many methods can be used for self-assessment. **Tools** recommended for assessment and self-assessment include the following: description/videotaping an exemplar performance; instructions to candidates and assessors; scenarios and outlines of roles and key steps or issues to be covered; a list of set questions or a bank of questions; a checklist for assessment; instructions/guidelines for designing questions; a marking scheme; model case studies for analysis, etc.

A detailed discussion of assessment/self-assessment strategies and tools in an academic setting in relation to work-integrating learning can be found in an article by Theresa Winchester-Seeto, Jacqueline Mackaway, Debra Coulson and Marina Harvey.

For practical purposes, most assessment/self-assessment procedures use criterion-referenced measures by matching the student's performance against a set of criteria and using a scoring scale (also known as **rubric**). A rubric typically consists of two components: criteria and levels of performance. As an example, you may want to take a look at the VALUE Rubric[35] developed by the Association of American Colleges and Universities. Some of their rubrics can be used for self-assessment, particularly, rubrics for Written and Oral Communication, Teamwork, Life-long Learning. The rubric for assessing teamwork[36] begins with a clear identification of what teamwork means and consists of five criteria (contribution to team meetings; facilitation of contribution to team meetings; individual contribution outside of team meetings; fostering constructive team climate and response to conflicts) and four performance levels with related descriptions of each level. Ideally, by using the rubric individuals are supposed not only to learn about expectations for skill acquisition and their current standing, but also receive a clear direction for improvement. Yet another example of a pre-designed rubric[37] is provided by CLA (Collegiate Learning Assessment).

The advantage of using a well-developed rubric, with extensive and explicit descriptors for levels of performance, is that expectations for skill acquisition are clearly formulated, consistent, and objective; the disadvantage is that an accurate assessment takes time and should be done consistently. That's why a simplified approach is sometimes used where instead of descriptors

---

[34] http://jobs.iabc.com/c/coaching/library/item.cfm?site_id=65&id=167
[35] http://www.aacu.org/value/rubrics/
[36] http://www.aacu.org/value/rubrics/Teamwork.cfm
[37] http://wp.stolaf.edu/ir-e/files/2013/07/CLAscores.pdf

only levels of performance are indicated (poor, good, excellent) or a nominal (yes-no) scale is used (**a checklist**). To understand how to construct and use a rubric, we recommend that you get familiar with Jon Mueller's Authentic Assessment Toolbox[38].

Using tools to assess/self-assess graduate employability skills

Universities promoting graduate employability skills in their graduates use e-portfolios to gather and organize evidence of skills acquisition and assessment/self-assessment rubrics for evaluation/feedback purposes. A good example [39]is presented by Deakin University in Australia where standard templates are provided to instructors and students to pinpoint and evidence achievement in critical skills areas such as communication skills, information technology skills, critical and analytical thinking, problem solving, working independently, teamwork, cross-cultural skills and diversity. The rubrics developed at Deakin can be used for self-assessment purposes. More complex, three dimensional rubrics based on academic standards are suggested for graduate skills assessment/self-assessment by Leigh Wood, Theda Thomas and Brendan Rigby.

A comprehensive long term project charged with making the match between university graduates and corporate employers is described in an article by Iris Berdrow and Frederick Evers (2011). The researchers defined a set of 17 skills combined in 4 distinct areas (managing self, communicating, managing people, mobilizing innovation and change) that captured the current base competencies necessary to succeed in a business career and then described a competency-based course (similar to this one) where students were required to develop their skills portfolio, perform self-assessment, work on a presentation of their skills and prepare a plan for improvement. Their self-assessment plan included 17 skills (learning, personal organization/time management, personal strengths, problem solving/analytic skills, interpersonal skills, listening, oral communication, written communication, coordinating, decision making, leadership/influence, managing conflict, planning and organizing, ability to conceptualize, creativity/innovation/change, risk taking, visioning), a description of elements of each competency, a simplified rubric for self-assessment, and provided room for self-reflection and goal setting for self-improvement.

How the approach taken in this course is different

In this course, we take a similar approach to the one described in the previous section; the difference is that in the above mentioned examples colleges deal with traditional age students' preparation and transition to work. Traditional age college students typically know significantly less about "real-world", competitive employment than adult students. That's why they are usually offered a broad spectrum of potentially useful employability skills derived for their consideration by researchers and professors; then, the students are asked to self-assess themselves based on their perceptions of mastery/preparedness in the suggested skills areas. As a proxy for future competitive selection experiences, this seems to be a valid approach, but still it is an academic exercise and is not the same as a real life experience. In this course we primarily target adult students, i.e. those with significantly more experience in gaining competitive employment. That's why we have suggested students to specify a description for the position that

---

[38] http://jfmueller.faculty.noctrl.edu/toolbox/
[39] https://www.deakin.edu.au/__data/assets/pdf_file/0004/19327/clo-rubric-aqf7.pdf

they are familiar with and are interested in and then to identify a list of selection criteria and related competencies/skills including critical skills areas for the particular job. The resultant lists of CSAs are individualized and supposed to include only those items that truly matter for the students to get the job in a real life setting. The advantage of this approach is that it is more practical and job-related; also, it requires students to concentrate on fewer, more important skills in their particular situation. The disadvantage is that we cannot use a cookie cutter approach and use ready-made lists of skills, with detailed definitions, descriptors and rubrics. Ideally, based on the materials presented in this content guide and suggested readings, you should be able to come up with a list and definitions of CSAs relevant to your particular situation, identify related competency elements, develop descriptors, collect evidence of their performance, identify benchmarks/best practices, design rubrics and conduct self-assessment. Once the students will have mastered this approach, they will be able to use it continuously for finding employment, getting promotion and self-improving.

The E-Portfolio task ET-3 in this Module is designed to help mastering self-assessment for use in a competitive environment. Assignment A3 is a reflective exercise that is designed to help organizing and explaining students' work to the instructor and to provide avenue for a constructive feedback.

3.4. Collecting evidence, identifying benchmarks, designing and implementing tools (EP-3 and A3 tasks)

In this section, we describe tasks that should be completed in your E-Portfolio and Learning Journal Workbook (EP-3), with the use of the suggested Self-Assessment Tool (SAT), and in your Assignment A3.

Step 1: Critical skills areas (CSA):

<Based on your Key Selection Criteria Statement in Module 2 (Assignment 2), list here 5-6 most important, critical skills areas for the position you described. For example, *Communication Skills*>

Step 2: Critical skills subareas (competencies or units of competency):

<Broad skills areas (such as Communication Skills, Information Technology Skills, etc.) are typically composed of a number of smaller subareas. For example, a broad skills area Communication Skills includes a set of subareas, such as *Written Communications*, *Oral Communications*, *Presentation*, etc.) For each of the specified above CSA, identify 2-3 corresponding subareas that are most relevant for the job you described in Module 2 Assignment 2 (Those subareas are referred to as competencies or units of competency).

Step 3: Elements of competency:

<Each unit of competency can be further decomposed to the level of elements, so that in order to master a competency one needs to master all or most of the elements. For example, the unit of competency Written Communication may include several elements, such as *Producing Memos*, *Executive Summaries*, *Analytical Reports*, etc. For each unit of competency specify 2-3 elements that you think are the most important to excel in the job you described in Module 2 Assignment 2>

Step 4: Evidence of your mastery in performing elements of competency:

<At this point, you are supposed to have specified 5-6 Critical Skills Areas, 10-18 Critical Skills Subareas (=Competencies, or Units of Competency) and a number of corresponding Elements of Competency (can be as few

as 10 or as many as 50). Review all elements of competency that you identified as the most important for the specified position and think about ways to describe/measure/demonstrate proficiency.   Provide a brief description/comment for each element of competency.

Step 5: Benchmarks/Best practices:

<Are you aware of standards/best practices in performing the specified above elements of competency that can be used as benchmarks? Provide some examples and if possible indicate where they can be found/observed>

Step 6: Self-assessment methods and techniques

<List self-assessment methods and techniques that you can use to benchmark your performance against other people's performance or standards>

Step 7: Self-assessment tests and results:

< This is time to practice self-assessment. For each Critical Skills Area, select 1-2 most important elements of competency, identify/design an appropriate self-assessment method (for example, rubric, checklist), select a piece of evidence of your performance and a benchmark/standard, and rate your performance against the benchmark/standard (1 –poor, 2- satisfactory, 3- good, 4 – excellent). Describe this exercise in detail in your Module 3 Assignment 3; provide a brief summary in E-portfolio and learning journal workbook >

Step 8: Self-assessment tool (SAT)

< Download a Self-Assessment Tool template, fill it in and submit as an attachment >

3.5. A note on competitive benchmarking

To get a meaningful result from the self-assessment exercise described in the previous section one has to take benchmarking very seriously. If benchmarking is done poorly or not adequately, the results of self-assessment wouldn't be sufficiently informative for developing an objective picture of the person's real standing. Neither will they help preparing for a competitive employment, nor will they provide with directions for an efficient self-improvement. That's why we have recommended taking an objective, external view on own skills repertoire and performance. But how can one increase the validity of benchmarking? Are there any lessons that can be taken from corporate benchmarking in the business world? Are there any models that are used by companies and organizations for self-assessment and can be used by individuals?

This is a highly interesting topic that we would like you to discuss in Discussion D3. How can a job seeker benefit from using proven business strategy methods and tools (for example, VRINE - or VRIO analysis) for self-assessment, and why? To learn more about VRIO analysis, you may use some of the popular strategic management resources like Strategic Management Insight.[40]

Let's see how a business strategist that is charged with conducting self-assessment of a company may approach the task. Usually, an educated strategist begins with identifying factors that are deemed to be critically important for the chosen industry/sector (also known as KSF – *key success factors*). KSF are those factors that are absolutely necessary *for any company* to succeed given the industry characteristics. For example, in the commercial aircraft industry any

---

[40] http://www.strategicmanagementinsight.com/tools/vrio.html

competitor must possess large amounts of capital and research and development capabilities as prerequisites; any company lacking those capabilities is doomed to fail. An elaborated KSF analysis is used to create a list of categories (dimensions) for benchmarking the company's capabilities against competitors. Once the list of KSFs is ready, the strategist will turn to internal analysis to identify the company's resources and capabilities. If you google <*strategic resources and capabilities analysis*>, you'll find several useful approaches and tools used in the corporate world for that purpose (for example, value chain analysis, distinctive and key competencies analysis, etc.). As a result of those analyses, a list of resources and capabilities ("skills") of the company in the given industry will appear. After that the strategist will engage in a meticulous benchmarking of the company's resources and capabilities against the industry standards/ best practices pinpointed earlier as KSFs. A very popular tool for benchmarking that is recommended for use in the corporate world is known as VRINE (or VRIO) analysis. VRINE is actually a sort of rubric (or a checklist) used for comparison with the industry's "gold standard"; for each of the company's resources and capabilities the strategist is supposed to find out if this resource (or capability) is truly Valuable, Rare, Inimitable, Non-Substitutable and Exploitable. Ideally only VRINE-tested resources and capabilities with the highest scores should be included into the company's SWOT analysis as its true internal strengths. As we see, by using models and tools such as KSF, VRINE, SWOT the strategist can produce an objective and informative self-assessment report demonstrating how the company given its resources and capabilities is prepared to match the competition.

3.6. Readings

1. Loacker, J. (2003). Taking Self-Assessment Seriously. *Essays on Teaching Excellence toward the Best in the Academy, 15(2)*. The Vanderbilt Center for Teaching. Available online at http://cft.vanderbilt.edu/files/vol15no2_self_assessment.htm
2. Ross, John A. (2006). The Reliability, Validity, and Utility of Self-Assessment. *Practical Assessment Research & Evaluation*, 11(10). Available online at: http://pareonline.net/getvn.asp?v=11&n=10. Accessed August 4, 2014.
3. *Australian Government, Department of Education, Employment and Workplace Relations* (2012). TAEASS502A Design and develop assessment tools. Available online at: https://training.gov.au/TrainingComponentFiles/TAE10/TAEASS502A_R1.pdf. Accessed August 4, 2014.
4. *National Quality Council (2009).* Guide for Developing Assessment Tools. Victoria, Australia. Available online at: http://www.nssc.natese.gov.au/__data/assets/pdf_file/0011/51023/Validation_and_Moderation_-_Guide_for_developing_assessment_tools.pdf. Accessed August 4, 2014.
5. Joe Mueller (2010). *Authentic Assessment Toolbox*. Available online at http://jfmueller.faculty.noctrl.edu/toolbox/. Accessed August 6, 2014.
6. Winchester-Seeto, T., Mackaway, J., Coulson, D. & Harvey, M. (2010). 'But how do we assess it?' An analysis of assessment strategies for learning through participation (LTP). *Asia-Pacific Journal of Cooperative Education*, 11(3), 67-91. Available online at http://www.apjce.org/files/APJCE_11_3_67_91.pdf. Accessed August 6, 2014.

7. Berdrow I., Evers F.T. (2011). Bases of competence: A framework for facilitating reflective learner-centered educational environments. *Journal of Management Education*, 35 (3), 406-427. Available online at: http://jme.sagepub.com.library.esc.edu/content/35/3/406.full.pdf+html. Accessed August 6, 2014.

8. Wood, L., Thomas, T., and Rigby, B. (2011). Assessment and standards for graduate outcomes. *Asian Social Science*, 7(4), 12-16. DOI: 10.5539/ass.v7n4p12. Available online at: http://ccsenet.org/journal/index.php/ass/article/view/9387. Accessed August 8, 2014.

Module 4: Self-Management
Module 4 Overview

The overarching goal of Module 4 is to organize findings and help students making sense of self-assessment with the use of a tool called Self-Assessed CSA Profile and Dashboard. Students are required to complete the process of self-assessment of their critical skills identified in previous Modules and enter this information into the dashboard; then, think about their demonstrated strengths and weaknesses, their competitive standing and reflect on their opportunities and threats. They may come up with ideas on self-developmental strategy building on strengths and eliminating weaknesses and the continuing use of a self-development lab. Then, we'll continue discussing the use of methods of business strategy for personal self-development concentrating on the issues of implementation and monitoring of the strategy. When examining the process for self-monitoring, motivating and reinforcing the strategy (self-programming), it's important to think about the practicality of the approach and learn from approaches to self-assessment developed in the career management and personnel development literature.

Learning Objectives of Module **4** are the following:

- Complete the process of self-assessment and present the findings using the Self-Assessed CSA Profile and Dashboard;

- Identify ways in which the results of self-assessment can be used for formulating individual career and learning goals and strategies;

- Examine how business entities implement and monitor their strategies and think about how similar approaches can be used for implementing and monitoring personal strategies;

- Review your progress towards achieving learning objectives of the course;

- Examine approaches to self-assessment recommended in career management and personnel development literature.

Learning Activities include:

- Readings and resources (this content guide and suggested additional sources);

- Discussion D4. How can we use "proven" business strategy methods and tools (for example, TOWS analysis or a balanced scoring card) for self-management, and why should we? You may start by discussing advantages of using business strategy for an organization. Then, read some suggestions by HR consultants (google <personal balanced score card>). Do you think that this kind of effort makes sense? What are advantages? Any associated problems? Can it be sustainable? In the long run?

- E-Portfolio task EP4;

- Written Assignment A4. Your task is to write a learning essay on the use of self-management tools and techniques for career development and personal growth. There are different ways to accomplish the task. You may want to continue working on the Module 3 essay and conduct a few more self-assessments. You may concentrate on developing your CSA Profile and Dashboard; this is a new comprehensive tool introduced in this course. Yet another approach would be to conduct a research and find out about other possible tools and models and even compare them. In particular, we would like you to think about how to make your self-assessment accurate and then how to make the best use of it.

Schedule and due dates (see Course Information Document).

4.1. Making sense of self-assessment

How to organize and present self-assessment results (E-Portfolio task ET-4)

In this section, we describe tasks that should be completed in your E-Portfolio and Learning Journal Workbook (EP-4), with the use of the suggested Self-Assessed CSA Profile and Dashboard Tool.

Step 1: A CSA profile: an example

<Download a Self-Assessed CSA Profile and Dashboard EXAMPLE (pdf), review it and read instructions>

Step 2. My CSA profile

<Download a Self-Assessed CSA Profile and Dashboard Template, fill it in based on the information collected in your Self-Assessment Tool (SAT) in Module 3 and the above example>

Step 3. Weighing Critical Skills Areas

<When considering applicants for a job, employers often weigh selection criteria. Oftentimes, but not always, the most relevant criteria are mentioned first in the job description. Think about the position you described in Module 2 assignment and assign weights to competencies. Make sure that the total of weights is 100. Then, an ideal candidate for the job will score 100 points. Now, you may calculate your score and your standing in relation to an ideal candidate. If, for example, the weight of Written Communications is 20 and your self-assessed performance level is 2 out of 4 (50%), then your score for Written Communications is 10. The more honest you are in your self-assessment, the more accurate picture of your real standing you'll get. In the example provided the total score of a prospective student is 66.5 which clearly indicate that there is plenty of room for growth. What is your score?>

Step 4. My CSA parities and gaps

<Now, you can visualize the whole picture of your employability skills in relation to the position you specified in Module 2 assignment. You can see where you are on par with the best candidates (your competitive parities) or even exceed expectations, but also where you fall behind and there are gaps in your preparation. Some gaps may be minor and some severe>

Step 5. My CSA dashboard

<Complete your Self-assessed CSA Profile and Dashboard and submit it as an attachment>

Your competitive standing

The idea behind the dashboard is to provide a user with a clear and honest picture of her/his real competitive standing in relation to potential candidates for the position specified in Module 2 Assignment 2.

If this is a job of your dream that you think you may be able to get at some point, your dashboard is supposed to tell you where you are and what needs to be done in order to improve your position in the future and get that or a similar job. What is particularly important is that your dashboard is not a product of wishful thinking, but on the contrary it is based on a solid evidentiary base of your own performance and best practices/standards in the field.

Identifying gaps and parities

The dashboard is designed to provide a clear picture of the person's strengths and weaknesses; as such, it can be very instrumental in the development of personal strategies aimed at building on strengths and eliminating weaknesses. For example, it demonstrates which particular skills and competencies can be considered demonstrated strengths and should be emphasized in the person's self-marketing and in a job application/interview (more in the next Module). Also, it tells about particular skills that needs improvement (more on self-development in Module 6).

How accurate is Dashboard?

Like any tool, Dashboard's accuracy completely depends on the quality of the information collected and self-assessment results obtained. There are two rather difficult tasks involved in constructing a personal dashboard including: a) identification of the relevant standards/best practices and obtaining examples and b) conducting the self-assessment. The question is whether students can do it on their own, without some (or significant help) from experienced academics, mentors, consultants, trainers. The whole idea of lifelong, self-directed learning is that in the 21st century the only way to succeed is to become self-independent, self-taught and self-managed. To do so, one needs to develop necessary competencies in self-regulated learning (see more in Modules 2 and 3). One of the characteristics of self-regulated learners is that they actively seek and know how to use constructive feedback from professionals and peers.

Assignment A4

Your task is to write a learning essay on the use of self-management tools and techniques for career development and personal growth. There are different ways to accomplish the task. You may want to continue working on the Module 3 essay and conduct a few more self-assessments. You may concentrate on developing your CSA Profile and Dashboard. Yet another approach would be to conduct research and find out about other possible tools and models and even compare them. In particular, we would like you to think about how to make your self-assessment accurate and then how to make the best use of it.

4.2. What can we learn from business strategy?

<u>From SWOT to formulating and implementing strategies (Discussion D4)</u>

Most organizations routinely do strategic planning, nevertheless only some succeed and some do not. One of the most difficult problems is how to scan the external environment correctly and come up with meaningful results; another problem is how to predict the future and prepare for that by developing necessary skills in advance. Suppose that one has got a kind of "crystal ball" to see the future and has developed an excellent strategy to excel in that future, how can she/he implement and sustain the strategy? Change is not easy, organizations are known to be subject of so called "path dependence" and routinely fail to implement strategies of change. So do individuals. We suggest that you discuss related issues in Discussion D4.

How can we use proven business strategy methods and tools (for example, TOWS analysis or a balanced scoring card) for self-management, and why should we? You may start by discussing advantages of using business strategy for an organization (take a look at the following website: http://www.s-m-i.net/pdf/Business%20strategy%20intro.pdf or just google <advantages of using business strategy>). Then, read some suggestions by HR consultants (google <personal balanced score card>). Do you think that this kind of effort makes sense? What are advantages? Any associated problems? Can it be sustainable? In the long run? How?

<u>A personal balanced scoring card</u>

To implement a strategy, organizations oftentimes use an instrument called "a balanced scoring card". As stated by the <u>Balanced Scorecard Institute</u>[41],

The balanced scorecard is a strategic planning and management system that is used extensively in business and industry, government, and nonprofit organizations worldwide to align business activities to the vision and strategy of the organization, improve internal and external communications, and monitor organization performance against strategic goals. It was originated by Drs. Robert Kaplan (Harvard Business School) and David Norton as a performance measurement framework that added strategic non-financial performance measures to traditional financial metrics to give managers and executives a more 'balanced' view of organizational performance. While the phrase balanced scorecard was coined in the early 1990s, the roots of the this type of approach are deep, and include the pioneering work of General Electric on performance measurement reporting in the 1950's and the work of French process engineers (who created the Tableau de Bord – literally, a "dashboard" of performance measures) in the early part of the 20th century.

Some management consultants suggested using the concept for self-management. You may find it useful to get familiar with the work of Hubert Rampersad, particularly, <u>the idea of using a personal balanced scorecard</u>[42]. A similar approach to personal balanced scoring card is presented in <u>a document</u>[43] created by Elena Salazar.

---

[41] http://balancedscorecard.org/Resources/About-the-Balanced-Scorecard
[42] http://marshallgoldsmithlibrary.com/docs/ThoughtLeaders/Rampersad/TPS-Aligning-Human-Capital.pdf
[43] http://www.reliability.com/industry/articles/Jun_12_08_Creating%20your%20PBSC_ES%20%282%29.pdf

Closing the loop: revising goals and skills

One of the important elements of corporate strategy-making is to continuously monitor the environment and if necessary revise goals and strategies. A similar approach can be taken for self-management based on the data presented in the Dashboard.

4.3. Developing an effective self-management strategy

Let's check what we've got so far

As mentioned earlier (Module 1), while the degree planning process at ESC is an excellent instrument for the identification of individual learning goals and curricular mapping in accordance with the requirements (i.e., for identifying the purpose of each study included into the student's individual DP), it doesn't provide students with a methodology/instruments to monitor and self-assess their progress in terms of the acquisition of graduate employability skills. Ideally, in addition to degree planning, students should be able to:

- Measure the outcomes of their studies, including levels of skills acquisition, in relation to job requirements;
- Identify and implement logical steps in their professional development;
- Be acutely aware of their competitive strengths and weaknesses and master self-marketing techniques.

This course is intended to provide students with the necessary methodology and tools and puts emphasis on self-management as the key meta-skill. In Modules 2-3 you have learned how to approach and conduct the foundational steps in self-management, namely self-analysis and self-assessment, in a business context. In particular, you have examined relevant psychological theories and concepts, methods and tools used by business strategists, and approaches to self-assessment suggested in vocational training literature. To combine theory and practice, you have identified your own professional and generic competencies and skills that seem to be most valued by employers in your chosen field; then, you have engaged in collecting relevant evidence of your actual mastery and performance and measured it against benchmarks. To do so, you have started using self-management tools like self-observation and self-reflection instruments (learning journal), self-assessment instruments (rubrics, checklists), monitoring tools (dashboard and e-portfolio). In Module 4 you are supposed to review and organize your findings to make sure that you can use self-management knowledge and skills to guide your ongoing professional development and personal growth in future.

Your personal lab

By now, we have introduced enough instruments to create a self-development lab. Does one really need to have a learning journal, an e-portfolio, a collection of evidence of your own performance and best practices, a range of tools for self-assessment, a collection of skill-builders, a monitoring device (dashboard)? Does it sound like another full time job? Do we have enough trouble without it?

A simple answer is that there are some tools that are continuously used in professional life anyway; for example, resumes, CVs, short bios, presentations, professional portfolios, LinkedIn accounts, references, diaries, self-help books, etc. The approach taken in this course builds on those practices and suggests a way to integrate various tools and take advantage of efforts of many theorists and practitioners concerned with the development of employability skills.

In a nutshell, your personal self-development lab is a place (real or imaginary) where you can pinpoint your skills and measure them against the competition to answer the following questions: What do I really know and what can I do? What can I do better than potential candidates and where should I improve? What are my real strengths and weaknesses? What are threats and opportunities? What are my options? How should I improve my skills? Which courses should I take and why? What level should I be able to achieve, why and how?

CSA dashboard: an instrument for self-management

In this course, we build on existing theories and reported approaches and suggest using certain self-assessments tools and a dashboard as a self-reporting and self-monitoring tool. It can certainly be further adjusted to individual needs. For example, some HR development consultants suggest using a personal balanced scoring card. The dashboard can easily be incorporated into this approach.

An interesting example of a self-development lab[44]

4.4. From self-management to managerial competencies

In this course, we do not cover the full range of employability skills that can be developed in an individual and are mostly interested in self-management, self-marketing and other personal skills (for example, communication skills, presentation skills). In the personnel development and career management literature there are many well-developed approaches to personnel assessment/self-assessment that can be used in a personal self-development lab. For example, University of Alabama created a model known as support professional competency[45] that includes self-assessment tools. The model includes areas of competency for student affairs' professionals and other categories, includes 2-3 levels of competency for each competency and works as a sort of dashboard where target skills are identified and professional development plans can be developed. A similar, but significantly more elaborated process of self-assessment[46] is developed by the Department of Human Services in Victoria, Australia. This document includes details for conducting self-assessment by personnel, explains self-assessment tools and criteria used, prescribes the process of self-assessment and the collection of evidence, identifies categories of evidence, and explains how evidence should be collected, assessed and rated. Yet another detailed document for assessment of managerial competencies that can also be used for self-assessment is presented in a report[47] prepared by the American Institutes for Research for

---

[44] http://www.rotman.utoronto.ca/FacultyAndResearch/ResearchCentres/DesautelsCentre/Programs/SDL.aspx
[45] http://www.sa.ua.edu/proDevCompetencyModels.cfm?p=7
[46] *www.dhs.vic.gov.au*
[47] http://www.pro-net2000.org/cm/content_files/71.pdf

the U.S. Department of Education. In this report, the authors provided descriptors for levels of competency for 21 managerial competencies and suggested ways to develop profiles for each competency based on rating available evidence; finally, they came up with a summary profile for each competency (an approach very similar to the one used in this course).

4.5. Readings and resources

1. *Professional Staff Competency Model & Self-Assessment Tool*. University of Alabama. Available online at: http://www.sa.ua.edu/documents/ProfDevelopPlan2012-13_000.xlsx. Accessed August 11, 2014.

2. *Department of Human Services Standards Self-Assessment Report and Quality Improvement Plan*. September 2012. Victoria, Australia. Available online at: http://www.dhs.vic.gov.au. Accessed August 11, 2014.

3. U.S. Department of Education (2002). *Management Competencies Assessment Instrument*. Available online at: www.pro-net2000.org/cm/content_files/71.pdf. Accessed August 11, 2014.

Module 5 Self-Marketing
Module 5 Overview

Learning Objectives of Module **5** are the following:

- Examine approaches to creating professional portfolios and self-marketing plans in competency-based academic programs;

- Review personal branding as a functional marketing strategy;

- Examine and discuss the use of social media for self-marketing and self-promotion;

- Examine your own presentation skills, develop and implement a rubric for self- and peer-assessment of your presentation skills.

Learning Activities include:

- Readings (this content guide and suggested additional sources);

- Discussion D5;

- E-Portfolio task EP5;

- Written Assignment A5.

Schedule and due dates (see Course Information Document).

5.1. Converting your strengths into selling points

From professional portfolio to self-marketing plan

In some competency-based and professionally oriented academic programs, developing a professional portfolio and a self-marketing plan is part of the students' preparation. An excellent example[48] is presented on the Excelsior College's website for their capstone course in the Master of Nursing program. This example is very useful to understand the underlying logic for building a self-marketing plan in any occupation. It begins with developing a comprehensive professional portfolio, and then continues with designing a realistic description for a desired type of job and a rationale for this job. After that it discusses the unique attributes of candidates' preparation and culminates with a demonstration of their individual skills.

---

[48] http://www.excelsior.edu/static/syllabus/rubrics/SON_Mod7Assignment_NUR514.pdf

Creating a personal brand

Your competitive strengths as reported in the Dashboard and supported by evidence in the e-portfolio need to be converted into unique selling points (USP). To do so, it is useful to find out about how generic strategies are usually implemented in the business world. Particularly, how generic strategies are supplemented by functional strategies, including marketing strategies. You may want to begin by googling <marketing strategy>. It is likely that you'll find out resources and articles on branding and brand management, including personal branding (an example[49]). We suggest that you discuss related issues in Discussion 5.

5.2. Presenting your personal brand to the world

The use of social media

Social media are now universally used for communication and self-promotion; we suggest that you discuss and practice the use of social media for self-marketing in Module 5. In addition, make sure that you find and read relevant scholarly sources, as this topic is being heavily researched. In particular, we suggest that you read the following articles. Jose van Dijck (2013) in his article discussed the problem of online identity formation comparing Facebook and LinkedIn. The use of LinkedIn for accounting and business students is discussed in a brief article by W. David Albrecht (2011). The effects of LinkedIn on deception in resumes are discussed in an article by Jamie Guillory and Jeffrey Hancock (2012).

Presentation skills

It is likely that presentation skills are one of the critical skills that are included into your Dashboard. You may use your presentation for a) self-assessing your skill; b) soliciting feedback from your peers. For any of these purposes you will need a rubric. Actually, it's good to have a valid presentation skills rubric in your personal lab anyway. To find one, you may want to google <presentation skills rubric>. There is always an underlying theory behind each rubric. To learn more you may want to read the following blog[50].

5.3. Combining it all together (E-portfolio tasks)

Step 1. Using your CSA Profile and Dashboard for self-promotion

<If your CSA Profile and Dashboard are all green, then you are perhaps the best candidate for the job. Or, maybe, your self-assessment was not honest or accurate. Or, you are overqualified and you should be thinking of getting a better job. Anyway, it is logical to capitalize on your green areas and promote yourself for prospective employers.

---

[49] http://www.today.com/id/44994555/ns/today-today_books/t/you-are-brand-strategic-approaches-self-promotion/#.U-oUgiiGdRo
[50] http://drsaraheaton.wordpress.com/2010/12/20/rubrics-for-grading-student-presentations/

To begin with, list your green areas (demonstrated competencies) here and compare with your earlier entries (My Career Summary, My Professional Skills, My Generic Skills).

Step 2. <u>Self-Marketing Strategies and Tools</u>

< How can one approach self-marketing using strategic tools and models such as SWOT, VRINE, a balanced scoring card? List here self-marketing strategies and tools that one may use for self-promotion.

Step 3. <u>"My self-marketing strategy"</u>

< What is your USP (unique selling proposition) for your prospective employer based on their needs and your strengths (demonstrated competencies)? Explain.

Step 4. "My presentation"

<There are many ways to present one's USP to get a job or promotion. Some of the widely used are a PowerPoint presentation, a personal website, an electronic portfolio (for example, a LinkedIn account, a Mahara e-portfolio), etc. You will be asked to present your USP in the format of your choice (Module 5 assignment).

Step 5. Self-Assessment Rubric

<As part of the Module 5 assignment, you'll be asked to design a self-assessment tool for your presentation.

5.4. Readings

1. Dijck, J. (2013). 'You have one identity': performing the self on Facebook and LinkedIn, *Media, Culture & Society, 35(2)*, 199-215. Available online at: http://mcs.sagepub.com.library.esc.edu/content/35/2/199.full.pdf+html. Accessed August, 12, 2014.

2. Albrecht, D., W. (2011). LinkedIn for Accounting nnd Business Students. *American Journal of Business Education, 4(10),* 39-42. Available online at: http://www.cluteinstitute.com/ojs/index.php/AJBE/article/view/6062/6140. Accessed August 12, 2014.

3. Guillory, J., and Hancock, J. (2012). The effects of LinkedIn on deception in resumes. *Cyberpsychology, Behavior and Social Networking, 15(3),* 135-140. DOI: 10.1089/cyber.2011.0389. Available online at: .http://eds.a.ebscohost.com.library.esc.edu/ehost/pdfviewer/pdfviewer?sid=650babc5-bd66-4c65-9190-ef8342886caa%40sessionmgr4002&vid=0&hid=4103. Accessed August 12, 2014.

Module 6: Self-Reflection and Self-Improvement
Module 6 Overview

Learning Objectives of Module **6** are the following:

- Re-examine the concept of self-directed learning skills;

- Review and discuss the role of constructive feedback and practice in receiving/providing peer-to-peer feedback;

- Examine the concept of transformative learning;

- Develop a professional development plan;

- Review your progress and reflect on your learning in this course.

Learning Activities include:

- Readings (this content guide and suggested additional sources);

- Discussion D6;

- E-Portfolio task EP6 and the Final Submission of the entire E-Portfolio;

- Written Assignment A6.

Schedule and due dates (see Course Information Document).

6.1. Self-directed learning skills

"My self-directed learning (SDL) skills" (E-portfolio task)

<Self-directed learning (SDL) is the foundational concept of this course. In Module 2 content guides you were introduced to the theme of self-regulated and self-directed learning. Now it's time to reflect and self-assess your SDL skills and perhaps add them to your CSA Profile and Dashboard and Professional Development Plan.

More on SDL skills

In the period of rapid changes SDL skills are among the most important skills; in order to stay current and to be competitive, one needs to know how to acquire new knowledge and skills and do it efficiently. At this point, we suggest that you read a few more articles on the topic. In 'Teach me How to Learn", Gregory Francom (2010) provided a brief review of literature on SDL and describes four main principles that can be derived from the literature. A previously quoted article by Andrea Ellinger (2004) provides detailed descriptions of SDL processes and implications for the workplace. Chris Patterson, Dauna Crooks and Ola Linyk-Child (2002) reported of an academic program in Canada where SDL skills and competencies were taught as part of the curriculum and described elements of competency and related rubrics for assessment/self-assessment.

Constructive feedback

Receiving an objective, motivating, accurate and constructive feedback is one of the cornerstones of self-regulated learning and skills development. In Discussion 6 we suggest that you provide feedback to your peers and receive feedback from them and discuss related issues.

Transformative learning

Developing SDL skills results in a major shift in someone's attitudes and behaviors; this is captured and described by transformative learning theory. The best way to familiarize with this theory is to google and read some of < Jack Mezirow's work on transformative learning>.

Professional Development Plan

Download the template, develop the plan and submit as an attachment. In developing you plans for the future you may want to think about stages of career development. As an example, a comprehensive model for the development of marketing professionals based on required skills and competencies at various stages (levels) was developed by Monash University in Australia and is described by Ian Walker (2009).

Self-Audit

Assignment 6 is designed as a self-audit. Please respond to the questions and provide your reflection.

6.2. Readings

1. Francom, G. M. (2011). Teach me how to learn: Principles for fostering students' self-directed learning skills. *International Journal of Self-Directed Learning, 7*(1), 29-44. Available online at: http://www.sdlglobal.com/IJSDL/IJSDL7.1-2010.pdf. Accessed August 12, 2014.
2. Ellinger, A. (2004). The Concept of Self-Directed Learning and Its Implications for Human Resource Development. *Advances in Developing Human Resources, 6(2)*, 158-177. DOI: 10.1177/1523422304263327. Available online at: http://adh.sagepub.com.library.esc.edu/content/6/2/158.short. Accessed August 12, 2014.

3. Patterson, C., Crooks, D., and Linyk-Child, O. (2002). A New Perspective on Competencies for Self-Directed Learning. *Journal of Nursing Education, 41(1)*, 25-31. Available online at: http://www.researchgate.net/publication/11518222_A_new_perspective_on_competencies_for_self-directed_learning. Accessed August 12, 2014.

4. Walker, I.,Tsarenko, Y., Wagstaff, P., Powell, I., Steel, M., and Jan Brace-Govan, J. (2009). The Development of Competent Marketing Professionals. Journal of Marketing Education, 31(3), 253-263. Available online at: http://jmd.sagepub.com.library.esc.edu/content/31/3/253.full.pdf+html. Accessed August 12, 2009).

Instructional Materials

Appendix 1

E-Portfolio and Learning Journal Workbook

E-Portfolio and Learning Journal Workbook

Student: _____ _____   ID number: _____
Area of Studies: BME (Business, Management & Economics)
Concentration: _____
Term, year: _____
Instructor: _____

Contents:

Module	Entries			Pages
	Designed for public viewing	**My personal lab**	**My Journal**	
1	My Summary /Resume My Work Experience	My Goals	Learning resources Notes	
2	My Professional Skills My Generic Skills	My Personal Characteristics	Learning resources Notes	
3	<Review Summary and Skills and revise if needed>	My Self-Assessment: - Critical Skills Areas/Subareas; - Evidence (examples of my work); - Benchmarks, best practices; - Self-assessment methods; - Self-assessment results.	Learning resources Notes	
4	<Review /revise Summary and Skills>	My CSA profile, gaps and parities My personal CSA dashboard	Learning resources Notes	
5	My Self-Presentation	My self-marketing strategy; My self-marketing tools	Learning resources Notes	
6	My Professional Development Plan	My SDL skills	Learning resources Notes	

Attachments:

✓ Module 1: Resume (CV)
✓ Module 3: Self-Assessment Tool (SAT)
✓ Module 4: Self-assessed CSA Profile and Dashboard
✓ Module 5: Self-presentation: a rubric for assessment
✓ Module 6: Professional development plan.

Module 1
Employability and Career Management Skills

"My Career Summary"

<Add here 4-6 lines to highlight your education, personal strengths, experiences, achievements, skills> Examples

"My Work Experience"

< This is a brief version of an extended Work Experience section that candidates usually include in their resume (Example). You should only include dates, companies, job titles, principal responsibilities and your major accomplishments>

"My Goals"

< Briefly describe your career goals (2-3 paragraphs)>. Examples.

"My resume"

You may type (or cut and paste your resume) in this document or add it as an attachment.

Module 1 (continued)

"My Learning Resources"

<Add 2-3 resources (books, articles, websites, blogs etc.) that can be useful for your ongoing professional development.

1.
2.
3.

"My Notes"

<Explain in 2-3 paragraphs main topics and ideas discussed in this Module. What have you learned?

ET-1 SUBMISSION:

When finished, submit this portion of the E-Portfolio and Learning Journal to your instructor in the designated box. You may submit the entire Workbook file. Due date: see Course Schedule.

Module 2
Self-Analysis Worksheet

"My Professional Skills"

<List here your professional skills (you can find definitions of professional skills in Module 1 content guides/resources>

"My Generic Skills"

<List here your generic skills (you can find definitions of generic skills in Module 1 content guides/resources>

"My Personal Characteristics"

< Describe your personal qualities and traits that you think can be transferred to your job. Examples.

Module 2 (continued)

"My Learning Resources"

<Add 6-8 resources (books, articles, websites, blogs etc.) that can be useful for your ongoing professional development.

1.
2.
3.
4.
5.
6.

"My Notes"

<Explain in 2-3 paragraphs main topics and ideas discussed in this Module. What have you learned?

ET-2 SUBMISSION:

When finished, submit this portion of the E-Portfolio and Learning Journal to your instructor in the designated box. You may submit the entire Workbook file. Due date: see Course Schedule.

Module 3
Self-Assessment Worksheets

Critical skills areas (CSA):

<Based on your Key Selection Criteria Statement in Module 2 (Assignment #2), list here 5-6 most important, critical skills areas for the position you described. For example, *Communication Skills*>

Critical skills subareas (competencies or units of competency):

<Broad skills areas (such as *Communication Skills, Information Technology Skills*, etc.) are typically composed of a number of smaller subareas. For example, a broad skills area *Communication Skills* includes a set of subareas, such as *Written Communications, Oral Communications, Presentation*, etc.) For each of the specified above CSA, identify 2-3 corresponding subareas that are most relevant for the job you described in Module 2 Assignment (Those subareas will be referred to as competencies or units of competency).

Elements of competency:

<Each unit of competency can be further decomposed to the level of elements, so that in order to master a competency one needs to master all or most of the elements. For example, the unit of competency *Written Communication* may include several elements, such as producing *Memos, Executive Summaries, Analytical Reports*, etc. For each unit of competency specify 2-3 elements that you think are the most important to excel in the job you described in Module 2 Assignment.>

Evidence of your mastery in performing elements of competency:

<At this point, you are supposed to have specified 5-6 Critical Skills Areas, 10-18 Critical Skills Subareas (=Competencies, or Units of Competency) and a number of corresponding Elements of Competency (can be in the range of 10-50). Review all elements of competency that you identified as important for the specified position and think about ways to describe/measure/demonstrate proficiency. Provide a brief description/comment for each element of competency.

Benchmarks/Best practices:

<Are you aware of standards/best practices in performing the specified above elements of competency that can be used as benchmarks? Provide some examples and if possible indicate where they can be found/observed>

Self-assessment methods and techniques

<List self-assessment methods and techniques that you can use to benchmark your performance against other people's performance or standards>

Self-assessment tests and results:

< This is time to practice self-assessment. For each Critical Skills Area, select 1-2 most important elements of competency, identify/design an appropriate self-assessment method (for example, *rubric, checklist*), select a piece of evidence of your performance and a benchmark/standard, and rate your performance against the benchmark/standard (1 –poor, 2- satisfactory, 3- good, 4 – excellent). Describe this exercise in detail in your Module 3 Assignment 3; provide here a brief summary.

Self-assessment tool (SAT)

< Download a Self-Assessment Tool template, fill it in and submit as an attachment>

Module 3 (continued)

"My Learning Resources"

Add 6-8 resources (books, articles, websites, blogs etc.) that can be useful for your ongoing professional development.

1.
2.
3.
4.
5.
6.

"My Notes"

Explain in 2-3 paragraphs main topics and ideas discussed in this Module. What have you learned?

Review "My Summary and Skills"

<Do you think that based on your self-assessment you will need to review/revise your Summary and Skills documents (modules 1-2). Explain and revise if needed.

ET-3 SUBMISSION:

When finished, submit this portion of the E-Portfolio and Learning Journal to your instructor in the designated box. You may submit the entire Workbook file. Due date: see Course Schedule.

Module 4
Self-Management Worksheets

A CSA profile: an example

<Download a Self-Assessed CSA Profile and Dashboard EXAMPLE (pdf), review it and read instructions

"My CSA profile"

<Download a Self-Assessed CSA Profile and Dashboard Template, fill it in based on the information collected in your Self-Assessment Tool (SAT) in Module 3 and the above example.

Weighing Critical Skills Areas

<When considering applicants for a job, employers often weigh selection criteria. Oftentimes, but not always, the most relevant criteria are mentioned first in the job description. Think about the position you described in Module 2 assignment and assign weights to competencies. Make sure that the total of weights is 100. Then, an ideal candidate for the job will score 100 points. Now, you may calculate your score and your standing in relation to an ideal candidate. If, for example, the weight of Written Communications is 20 and your self-assessed performance level is 2 out of 4 (50%), then your score for Written Communications is 10. The more honest you are in your self-assessment, the more accurate picture of your real standing you'll get. In the example provided the total score of a prospective student is 66.5 which clearly indicates that there is plenty of room for growth. What is your score?

"My CSA parities and gaps"

<Now, you can visualize the whole picture of your employability skills in relation to the position you specified in Module 2 assignment. You can see where you are on par with the best candidates (your competitive parities) or even exceed expectations, but also where you fall behind and there are gaps in your preparation. Some gaps may be minor and some severe.

My CSA dashboard"

<Complete your Self-assessed CSA Profile and Dashboard and submit it as an attachment.

Module 4 (continued)

"My Learning Resources"

< Add 6-8 resources (books, articles, websites, blogs etc.) that can be useful for your ongoing professional development.
1.
2.
3.
4.
5.
6.

"My Notes"

Explain in 2-3 paragraphs main topics and ideas discussed in this Module. What have you learned?

Review "My Summary and Skills"

<Do you think that based on your self-assessment you will need to review/revise your Summary and Skills documents (modules 1-2). Explain and revise if needed.

ET-4 SUBMISSION:

When finished, submit this portion of the E-Portfolio and Learning Journal to your instructor in the designated box. You may submit the entire Workbook file. Due date: see Course Schedule.

Module 5

Self-Marketing Worksheets

Using your CSA Profile and Dashboard for self-promotion

<If your CSA Profile and Dashboard is all green, then you are perhaps the best candidate for the job. Or, may be, your self-assessment was not honest or accurate. Or, you are overqualified and you should be thinking of getting a better job. Anyway, it is logical to capitalize on your green areas and promote yourself for prospective employers. To begin with, list your green areas (demonstrated competencies) here and compare with your earlier entries (My Career Summary, My Professional Skills, My Generic Skills).

Self-Marketing Strategies and Tools

< How can one approach self-marketing using strategic tools and models such as SWOT, VRINE, a balanced scoring card? List here self-marketing strategies and tools that one may use for self-promotion.

"My self-marketing strategy"

< What is your USP (unique selling proposition) for your prospective employer based on their needs and your strengths (demonstrated competencies)? Explain.

"My presentation"

<There are many ways to present one's USP to get a job or promotion. Some of the widely used are a PowerPoint presentation, a personal website, an electronic portfolio (for example, a LinkedIn account, a Mahara e-portfolio), etc. You will be asked to present your USP in the format of your choice (Module 5 assignment).

Self-Assessment Rubric

<As part of the Module 5 assignment, you'll be asked to design a self-assessment tool for your presentation.

Module 5 (continued)

My Learning Resources:

Add 6-8 resources (books, articles, websites, blogs etc.) that can be useful for your ongoing
professional development.

1.
2.
3.
4.
5.
6.

My Notes:

Explain in 2-3 paragraphs main topics and ideas discussed in this Module. What have you
learned?

Review "My Summary and Skills"

<Do you think that based on your self-assessment you will need to review/revise your Summary
and Skills documents (modules 1-2). Explain and revise if needed.

ET-5 SUBMISSION:

**When finished, submit this portion of the E-Portfolio and Learning Journal to your instructor
in the designated box. You may submit the entire Workbook file. Due date: see Course
Schedule.**

Module 6
Using Self-Reflection for Self-Improvement

Peer-reviews of your work

<All students' presentations will be available for viewing in Module 6 discussion where you'll be asked to provide feedback and conduct peer-assessment. What are your thoughts about peer-assessment of your work? Were you able to communicate your USP? Why?

Using your CSA Profile and Dashboard for self-improvement

<If your CSA Profile and Dashboard is all yellow and red, then you will perhaps have a hard time getting the job. Or, may be, when doing self-assessment you were too harsh to yourself. Anyway, areas highlighted yellow and red are supposed to signal that major improvements are required. Here you may list those areas.

"My professional development plan"

< Download and complete the Professional Development Plan Template and submit it as an attachment.

"My self-directed learning (SDL) skills"

<Self-directed learning (SDL) is the foundational concept of this course. In Module 2 content guides you were introduced to the theme of self-regulated and self-directed learning; also, we recommended you to read two articles (by J. Mezirow and E. Zimmerman). Now it's time to reflect and self-assess your SDL skills and perhaps add them to your CSA Profile and Dashboard and Professional Development Plan.

Module 6 (continued)

"My Learning Resources"

Add 6-8 resources (books, articles, websites, blogs etc.) that can be useful for your ongoing professional development.

1.
2.
3.
4.
5.
6.

"My Notes"

Explain in 2-3 paragraphs main topics and ideas discussed in this Module. What have you learned?

Review "My Summary and Skills"

<Do you think that based on your self-assessment you will need to review/revise your Summary and Skills documents (modules 1-2). Explain and revise if needed.

Self-Audit:

Overall, what have you learned in this course? Think about it when responding to the Module 6 assignment questions.

FINAL SUBMISSION:

Review and submit the completed Workbook in the designated box. Due date: See Course Schedule.

If you have developed a supporting website in Mahara, submit the secure URL for review and request extra credit (up to 5%).

Templates

Appendix 2

Assignment 2: Position Description and Key Selection Criteria Statement

Assignment 2: Position Description and Key Selection Criteria Statement

Your Name _____ _____   Term, year _____

Organization

<Add a paragraph here briefly describing an organization (either real or fictional) that you would like to use as an example of a prospective employer in this assignment>

Position Title and Summary

<Add a paragraph here describing a job/position (either real or fictional) that you would like to get with the above organization in near future. Think about a position where the incumbent is required to have a college degree and a range of prerequisite skills>

Key Responsibilities

<Specify 6-8 key duties/responsibilities that will best describe the above position>

Key Selection Criteria*

To prepare a sound job application for the above position, applicants are required to briefly address EACH element of the Selection Criteria. You are allowed to modify some of the criteria as you see appropriate.

1. **Communication skills:** Demonstrated excellent written and oral communication skills, with the ability to prepare business memos, analytical reports, executive summaries and conduct oral presentations.
2. **Information management:** Experience/understanding of information technology and systems appropriate to the chosen field (*you may further specify this criterion*)
3. **Knowledge of business, management and economics:** Demonstrated ability to understand and solve problems using economic (*accounting, finance, HRM, management, marketing — please specify*) concepts and essential tools and techniques; a proven capacity to analyze and solve business problems from a range of disciplinary perspectives
4. **Ethical and social responsibility**: Demonstrated commitment to and appreciation for legal, ethical and social issues related to the chosen field.
5. **Analytical and problem solving skills:** Well developed analytical, problem solving skills and a demonstrated understanding of quantitative tools appropriate to the chosen field.

6. **Understanding people in an organizational context:** Demonstrated skills in developing and managing relationships with a diverse range of stakeholders and cross-functional teams.

7. **Understanding organizations within broader contexts:** An ability to effectively function in a complex and changing world and adapt to diversity, political, international, technological or environmental issues.

8. **Personal, interpersonal skills and attitudes:** A demonstrated ability to lead and manage a team in an area of high volume and high intensity workload; excellent planning, organizing and time management skills, with the ability to balance competing work priorities.

9. **Self-directed and active learning skills:** A capacity to assess and build upon previous experiences to pursue lifelong learning and professional growth goals, independently and in collaboration with others.

INSTRUCTIONS:

1. *Your task is to prepare a job application for the above position in the best possible way.*

2. *Specify Organization, Position Title/Summary and Key Responsibilities as you see appropriate.*

3. *Your paper will include: a) a modified Position Description; 2) a Covering Letter; 3) a detailed Selection Criteria Statement. You may also want to attach a resume.*

4. *The main part of this assignment is to write a detailed Selection Criteria Statement to address ALL Key Selection Criteria; think about how you can support your statements with evidence (at this point you are not required to provide evidence but you may use examples). This part of your assignment should be written on 4-5 pages (formatted, 1.5-spaced and proofread).*

5. *Please do not skip any criterion; if you think that a certain criterion is not relevant, explain why. If you think that it is relevant, but you haven't mastered it yet, explain how you can do it.*

6. *When finished, submit your work in the designated box in the .doc (.docx, .rtf) format.*

Appendix 3

Assignment 3: Self-Assessment Tool Template

Appendix 3

Assignment 3: Self-Assessment Tool Template

Student Name: _____

Term, Year: _____

1	2	3	4	5	6	7
Critical Skills Areas (CSA)	CSA Subareas (competencies)	Elements of competency	Evidence on file	Self-Assessment methods and techniques	Benchmark	Self-Assessment results (rating)
Example: **Communication skills**	Example: Written communications	Example: - Memo; - Executive Summary; - Analytical report; - <add>	Example: - A sample memo; - A sample summary; - A sample paper. - <add>	Example: - Checklist; - Expert (peer) observation; - Extended Rubric; - <add>	Example: - Model samples in a handbook	- 1 -poor; - 2 - satisfactory; - 3 - good; - 4 —excellent.
	<add>					
	<add>					
<add>	<add>					
<add>	<add>					
<add>	<add>					
<add>	<add>					
<add>	<add>					
<add>	<add>					
<add>	<add>					

INSTRUCTIONS:

7. This Self-Assessment Tool Template is designed to help you develop your personal Self-Assessment Tool (Module 3)
8. Your personal Self-Assessment Tool (SAT) should be designed based on Critical Skills Areas that you identify in Module 3 (see Workbook)
9. In Column 1 enter Critical Skills Areas (no less than 5 and no more than 8). For example, Communication Skills.

10. In Column 2 for each CSA enter 1-3 corresponding Critical Skills Subareas (=Competencies, or Units of Competency). For example, for Communications Skills you can enter Written Communications, Presentation skills, Oral Communications (depending on the requirements of the position you have specified in Module 2 Assignment)

11. In Column 3 enter Elements of Competency (i.e., single elements, activities that constitute a competency; in order to master a competency, one needs to master all or most elements). For example, for Written Communications elements can be a memo, an analytic report, etc.

12. In Column 4 you have to identify kinds of evidence that you are going to use in order to assess your level of mastery of each element of competency. For example, in order to assess your ability to write analytical reports, you'll have to present a report written by you.

13. In Column 5 you have to suggest a method or technique for each piece of evidence entered in Column 4

14. In Column 6 identify a benchmark, standard or a sample of best practice that can be used for self-assessment

15. In Column 7 write down the results of your self-assessment. Those ratings will be used for the CSA Profile and Dashboard in Module 4

16. When done with this Self-Assessment Tool, save and submit it as an attachment to ET-3 E-portfolio assignment (Module 3.)

Appendix 4

Assignment 4: Self-Assessed CSA Profiler and Dashboard

Appendix 4

Assignment 4: Self-Assessed CSA Profiler and Dashboard

Student Name: _____ Term, Year: _____

	Communication Skills		Interpersonal Skills		Analytic Skills		Diversity	IT Skills		SDL	
R	Written	Presentation	Teamwork	Leadership	Quantitative	Problem solving	Cross-cultural skills	Hardware, software	Technical writing	SDL skills	
1	●				●						
2				●			●			●	
3						●		●	●		
4		●	●								
W	20%	10%	10%	10%	10%	10%	10%	10%	6%	4%	100%
S	10	10	10	5	2.5	7.5	5	10	4.5	2	66.5
P											
G											

R - Rating (1 – poor, 4 – excellent), W – Weight (to reflect the importance of the skill), S – individual score, P – Parity, G – Gap (minor or severe)

INSTRUCTIONS:

17. This Template is designed to help you develop your personal Self-Assessed CSA Profile and Dashboard (Modules 4-6)

18. Your personal CSA Profile and Dashboard should be based on your self-assessment results (Column 7, SAT, Module 3).

19. The first step is to enter Critical Skills Areas and Subareas (competencies) from your personal SAT (Module 3).

20. You'll have to aggregate self-assessment results (ratings) obtained in your personal SAT in Module 3 (Column 7) to calculate a composite rating for each Critical Skills Subarea (competency). For example, if your Written Communication competency includes three elements of competency (Memo, Executive Summary and Analytic Report) and self-assessment results for those elements of competency are 3, 1 and 2 respectively, you'll have to come up with an aggregate rating which in your case is probably close to 2. Then, you need to enter this composite rating into the table and repeat for all Critical Skills Areas/Subareas. As a result, you'll receive your CSA Profile. Please note that CSA Profile is not constant; it will be different for each position and very much depend on your choice of standards/benchmarks and accuracy of your self-assessment.

21. The next step is to weigh the importance of each Critical Skill Subarea/competency included into the CSA Profile. The total of weights equals 100 (for an ideal candidate). Your individual score depends on your aggregated performance (rating) in each of the competencies (see Workbook for more detail).

22. The final step is to visualize your results. Green color is used to mark situations where your performance is close to the benchmark or standard; yellow is used to highlight the Critical Skills Subareas where improvement is required. Red light is meant to tell you about the subareas where your attention is required in the first place.

23. When your CSA Profile and Dashboard is completed, submit it as an attachment to Module 4 ET-5 E-portfolio assignment.

24. In Module 5 you will learn how to build self-promotional strategies based on the green areas. In Module 6 you will develop a 2-3 year professional development plan to address the red and yellow areas.

Appendix 5

E-Portfolio Task ET-6: Professional Development Plan

E-Portfolio Task ET- 6: Professional Development Plan

Student Name: _____   Term, Year: _____

1	2	3	4	5	6
Critical Skills Subareas	**Identified gaps in elements**	**Description**	**Action Items for self-improvement**	**Targets**	**Importance, timing**
Example: **Written Communications**	*Example:* Analytical reports *Rating 2 (out of 4)*	*Example:* As reflected in the rubric for analytical reports and peer-assessment, I scored low in the following categories: developing a sound argument, the use of evidence, the use of formats and styles	*Example:* 1. Take an advanced writing class, with an emphasis on report writing; 2. Discuss my skills gap with an expert, ask for advice and expert evaluation. 3. Work with the mentor.	Year 1: Rating 3 Year 2: Rating 4	#1 <add dates here>
	<add>				
	<add>				
	<add>				
<add>	<add>				
<add>	<add>				
<add>	<add>				
<add>	<add>				
<add>	<add>				
<add>	<add>				

INSTRUCTIONS:

1. This Professional Development Plan (PDP) Template is designed to help you develop your personal PDP (Module 6)
2. Your personal PDP should be based on the results of your self-assessment reported in the CSA Profile and Dashboard (Module 4)
3. In Column 1 enter Critical Skills Subareas (competencies) that are highlighted yellow or red in your CSA Profile and Dashboard
4. In Column 2 specify elements of competency that were rated low in your self-assessment (Module 3)
5. In Column 3 provide short descriptions of your CSA gaps based on your self-assessment

6. In Column 4 suggest a list of concrete steps (action items) to address CSA gaps

7. In Column 5 set targets in a 2-3 year perspective

8. In Column 6 identify the level of importance of this particular Critical Skills Subarea for your self-improvement; also, indicate when and how you are going to engage in activities specified in Column 4

When done with this form, submit as an attachment to Module 6 ET-6 E-portfolio assignment

Appendix 6

Assignment 1: Pre-Test Self-Audit

Appendix 6

Assignment 1: Pretest Self-Audit

Student: _____
Area of Studies: BME (Business, Management & Economics)
Term, year: _____

ID number: _____
Concentration: _____
Instructor: _____

Task 1: Answer questions 1-12 by assigning levels of importance and provide a brief rationale.

A) Little important; B) somewhat important; C) quite important; D) critically important.

#	Question	A	B	C	D	Your response
	How important do you think each of the following is to the employment success of new graduates of the degree program in your chosen field (concentration)?					Why do you think so? Please explain each answer in 2-3 sentences
1	Writing clearly and effectively					
2	Speaking clearly and effectively					
3	Thinking critically and analytically					
4	Analyzing quantitative problems					
5	Using information technology					
6	Working effectively with others					
7	Learning effectively on your own					
8	Understanding people of other racial and ethnic backgrounds					
9	Understanding different social contexts					
10	Developing a personal code of values and ethics					
11	General industry awareness					
12	Overall work-readiness					

Task 2: Answer questions 13 – 24 by assigning levels of your perceived achievement and provide brief comments.

A) Little; B) somewhat; C) quite a bit; D) very much.

#	Question	A	B	C	D	Your response
	To what extent has your experience during your ESC studies contributed to your personal development in the following?					Can you prove it? Please explain your answer in 2-3 sentences.
13	Writing clearly and effectively					
14	Speaking clearly and effectively					
15	Thinking critically and analytically					
16	Analyzing quantitative problems					
17	Using information technology					
18	Working effectively with others					
19	Learning effectively on your own					
20	Understanding people of other racial and ethnic backgrounds					
21	Understanding different social contexts					
22	Developing a personal code of values and ethics					
23	General industry awareness					
24	Overall work-readiness					

Notes:

1. Please answer honestly. The grade for this assignment is solely based on the timeliness and fullness of your response (do not skip questions).
2. This task is based on a modified *Graduate Employability Indicators Graduate Survey* originally designed by Dr. Beverley Oliver (http://api.ning.com/files/h4dIOCgKcHjJB7iiaWrE2R2gMkJLiTZeWaTi5Bizpk1wch-BygzWKTBUYWDerVw3*YdoSl2nnwG*nwT1cEkRlql0G2NETHmQ/fshiptwopager15may.pdf). Accessed 29 July, 2014

Appendix 7

Assignment 6: Post-Test Self-Audit

Assignment 6: Posttest Self-Audit

Student: _____

Area of Studies: BME (Business, Management & Economics)

Term, year: _____

ID number: _____

Concentration: _____

Instructor: _____

Task 1: Answer questions 1 – 12 by assigning levels of perceived adjustment needs and provide brief comments.

B) Little or not at all; B) somewhat; C) quite a bit; D) very much.

#	Question	A	B	C	D	Your response How do you know that? Please explain your answer in 2-3 sentences.
	Could (should) your degree program at ESC be changed (adjusted, supplemented by extracurricular activities) to improve your skills for employment including the following competencies:					
1	Writing clearly and effectively					
2	Speaking clearly and effectively					
3	Thinking critically and analytically					
4	Analyzing quantitative problems					
5	Using information technology					
6	Working effectively with others					
7	Learning effectively on your own					
8	Understanding people of other racial and ethnic backgrounds					
9	Understanding different social contexts					
10	Developing a personal code of values and ethics					
11	General industry awareness					
12	Overall work-readiness					
	Other skills and competencies (add more items if needed)					

Task 2: Answer questions 1-12 by assigning levels of achievement and provide a brief rationale.

B) Very little or not at all; B) somewhat; C) quite a bit; D) Very significantly.

#	Question	A	B	C	D	Your response — Why do you think so? Please explain each answer in 2-3 sentences
	As a result of this course, do you think that you:					
1	Developed a better understanding of employability skills?					
2	Developed a better understanding of self-management and self-marketing concepts and theories?					
3	Can use strategic models (like, SWOT, VRINE, etc.) for your personal development?					
4	Have mastered the use of self assessment tools and techniques?					
5	Can realistically evaluate your own skills and capabilities against competition?					
6	Can design a sound plan for your own professional development?					
7	Can implement the plan in real life?					
8	Can systematically use an e-portfolio for professional development?					
9	Have become a strategic, self-directed learner?					
10	Overall, was this course useful?					
11	What were the best aspects of this course?					
12	Where can we improve?					

Notes:

3. Please answer honestly. The grade for this assignment will solely be based on the timeliness and fullness of your response (do not skip questions).

4. Task 1 is based on a modified *Graduate Employability Indicators Graduate Survey* originally designed by *Dr. Beverley Oliver* (http://api.ning.com/files/h4dlOCgKcHiJB7iiaWrE2R2gMkJLiTZeWaTJ5Bizpk1wch-BygzWKTBUYWDerVw3*YdoSl2nnwG*nwT1cEkRlqiIOG2NETHmQ/fshiptwopager15may.pdf). Accessed 29 July, 2014

Appendix 8

Learning Activities at a Glance

Learning Activities

Week	Module theme, readings	Discussions (24%)	Assignments (50%) +Quizzes	E-Portfolio and Journal (26%)
	Everything labelled red will be developed later! Lectures: for all groups, guest lecturers and FAQ responses (a commons website or Coursera)	Q&A Self-Help Forum on the use of Mahara e-portfolios (remains open during the course, non-graded)	Quizzes: self-paced, until done A1, A6 – self-administered tests (10%) A2-A5 – graded assignments (40%)	E-Portfolio tasks ET 1-4 (10%) Final submission (16%) The use of Workbook is mandatory!
1,2	M1: Employability skills (Lecture 1) 21 century skills; career management; employability skills: e-portfolios	D1: Employability skills in the 21st century (IT, competition, globalization) (4%)	A1: Self-Audit pre-test* (5%) Quiz 1: Employability skills	ET1: 1) My summary/resume; 2) My work experience; 3) My goals; 4) My learning resources and notes (2%)
3,4	M2: Self-Analysis (Lecture 2) Theory: SRL and SDL, styles, motivation, metacognition. Competitive environment. A personal SWOT analysis	D2: Conducting a personal SWOT analysis: Strategic approach to self-development (4%)	A2: Essay. A selection criteria statement (10%) Quiz 2: Self-Analysis	ET2: 5) My professional skills; 6) My generic skills; 7) My personal characteristics. Add to 4). (2%)
5,6,7	M3: Self-Assessment (Lecture 3) Performance criteria, basics of assessment, self-assessment tools; benchmarks	D3: "Measuring performance: evidence, benchmarks, best practices, models, using VRINE model (4%)	A3: Essay. Collecting/documenting evidence, conducting self-assessment (10%) Quiz 3: Self Assessment	ET3: 8) Critical skills areas (CSA) and subareas; 9) Elements of competency; 10) Evidence; 11) Benchmarks; 12) Self-assessment methods; 13) results. Add to 4). (2%)
8,9, 10	M4: Self-Management (Lecture 4) Understanding CSA gaps Methods: A personal scoring card	D4: "Self-management strategies and models: a personal balanced scoring card, TOWS (4%)	A4: Essay. Making sense of self-assessment, dashboard (10%) Quiz 4: Self Management Skills	ET4: 12) My KSA profile; 13) My CSA gaps and parities; 14) My dashboard. Review/revise 1), 5), 6). Add to 4). (2%)
11, 12, 13	M5: Self-Marketing (Lecture 5) 4P of Self-Marketing	D5: "Self-Marketing strategies: Using social media (LinkedIn) for self-promotion" (4%)	A5: PPT + Notes: "USP" (10%) Quiz 5: Self Marketing Skills Coded finished works are made viewable for peer-assessment	ET5: 15) My self-marketing skills and strategies. Add to 4). (2%)

14, 15	M6: Self-Presentation, Peer-Assessment and Self-Reflection; Planning for Improvement (Lecture 6) Read: Presentation skills: peer assessment Methods: Lifelong learning: How to endure	D6: **Peer-assessment of 2-3 presentations.** How can you advise and what have you learned? (4%)	A6 (week 15): **Self-Audit post-test*** (5%) Comments and reflections on learning. A7 (week 15): Present your job application via Blackboard Collaborate for the panel (all students)	ET6: 16) My SDL skills; 17) My PD Plan. Add to 4). Review and submit your e-portfolio Word file with all attachments **(16%)** Using **Mahara** is optional 5% extra credit

Comments:

1) Self-Audit* pre-and post-test* surveys are intended to capture the student's learning in the course (SQSL type of scale).

2) A **Selection Criteria Statement**** is a key document for a fictional job search that requires applicants to write an essay addressing Selection Criteria. Selection Criteria are written based on the BME general guidelines; we'll have to further specify the guidelines using specific job advertising language (for example, asking for oral, written, executive communication skills, with the use of various media). The statement will be used by students to identify their **CSA gaps.**

3) An **e-portfolio:** is a structured tool to document self-development and collect evidence supporting the selection criteria statement, evaluate it and use for continuous self-improvement, as well as for self-promotion; also, a self-reflection tool (**learning journal**). We'll be using a Word template (Mahara is optional for extra credit)

4) Based on their e-portfolios, students will create a self-promotional **Presentation** (a PPT and supplementary notes). Those materials will be coded and used for peer-assessment; also, for a live mock job interview session via Blackboard Collaborate (presenters will receive extra credit?)

5) In the end, students will finalize their **learning journals** and draft a 2-3 **professional development plan** addressing CSA gaps and suggesting strategies and resources.

A Sample Course Description

BME-214524 Self-Management and Self-Marketing

Upper level, liberal, 4 credits

This 4-credit, 15-week course is designed to provide students with theoretical knowledge and practical, job-related skills in self-management and self-marketing. Students will learn how to use contemporary learning theories and fundamental management and marketing concepts to guide their self-and career development. Throughout the course, students will engage in a series of learning activities aimed at developing, documenting, evaluating, peer-reviewing, presenting and improving their practical self-management and self-marketing competencies and skills. They will learn how to use e-portfolios for conducting their personal SWOT analysis and self-assessment and will use social media tools to support their ongoing personal and professional development; in addition, they should be prepared to participate in a live, peer-reviewed, mock job interview session conducted via a video-conferencing system. Overall, this course will foster students' self-awareness and self-reflection and will help them develop effective strategies for self-improvement and self-promotion.

As an educational planning study within the BME area, the course will be useful for BME students in any concentration; depending on the individual degree program design, it can be placed either as part of their concentration, or general learning. During the course, students will be required to present and evaluate concrete evidence of essential skills in all areas specified in the BME general guidelines; this activity is intended to strengthen the students' focus on learning outcomes of their college studies. This study can be taken at any point during the degree provided that prerequisite requirements are met. Students can discuss issues of timing with mentors. The advantage of taking it earlier (and before they finalize their degree plans) is that they should be better able to identify and understand their essential skills' gaps and then calibrate their ESC studies to address those deficiencies and build a stronger competency base. The advantage of taking it at a later stage is that they will have the opportunity to evaluate their progress and think proactively about their future self-improvement and career goals, including, but not limited to, graduate study.

Note: CDL matriculated students can use this course as part of their Educational Planning credit. Prerequisites: Foundational courses in principles of marketing and principles of management or equivalent knowledge/experience and upper level critical thinking skills.

Source: http://www.esc.edu

Made in the USA
Charleston, SC
02 September 2015